New Light *on the* ATONEMENT

REVELATIONS OF THE PROPHET JOSEPH SMITH ON THE ATONEMENT OF CHRIST

New Light on the ATONEMENT

Chad Morris

REVELATIONS OF THE PROPHET JOSEPH SMITH ON THE ATONEMENT OF CHRIST

CFI
Springville, Utah

ISBN 13: 978-1-55517-980-9
ISBN 10: 1-55517-980-0

Published by CFI, an imprint of Cedar Fort, Inc., 2373 W. 700 S., Springville, UT, 84663
Distributed by Cedar Fort, Inc., www.cedarfort.com

LIBRARY OF CONGRESS CATALOGING-IN-PUBLICATION DATA

Morris, Chad.
   New light on the Atonement / by Chad Morris.
      p. cm.
   Includes bibliographical references.
   ISBN 1-55517-980-0
   1. Atonement—Mormon Church. 2. Atonement—Church of Jesus Christ of Latter-day Saints.
I. Title.

   BX8643.A85M67 2006
   232'.3--dc22

                                             2006029169

Cover design by Nicole Williams
Cover design © 2006 by Lyle Mortimer
Edited and typeset by Angela Olsen

Printed in the United States of America

10 9 8 7 6 5 4 3 2 1

Printed on acid-free paper

Dedication

To Shelly and my children.

Acknowledgments

Thank you to my wife Shelly, for her great patience, constant encouragement, and many sacrifices. Thanks to my mom and dad for teaching me about the Savior and Joseph Smith for as long as I can remember. Thanks to my family, friends, and coworkers for their support and encouragement.

Thank you to Jeffery Marsh, Keith Wilson, and John Livingstone, for their time and insightful suggestions. Thanks also to Richard Bennett for his encouragement to explore this topic. Thanks also to Richard Cowan, Robert Millet, Kelly Ogden, and Paul Peterson for their help and counsel. Thanks to all those at Cedar Fort.

Table of CONTENTS

Chapter 1

A FOUNDATION THAT WILL REVOLUTIONIZE THE WORLD

THE EXHAUSTED APOSTLES TRIED IN VAIN to stay awake. Only a short distance away, Jesus Christ, the Son of God, and Creator of the universe fell on his face in agony. After several hours, Judas brought a band of armed of men to arrest the Prince of Peace. The Jewish high priests tried and found the Redeemer guilty. The priests then brought him before Pilate, who gave into the angry mob that cried for Christ's crucifixion. Jesus was forced to carry His own cross, bearing His sentence and public shame. Roman soldiers nailed Him to the large beam. His mother watched as He gave His life. Three days later, the unprecedented and almost unbelievable happened. Jesus Christ resurrected from the dead. He lived again.

Ever since the days of the mortal Jesus Christ, scholars, preachers, and laymen have had much to say about His death and Resurrection. Library shelves are filled with volumes expressing different views and commentary on the subject. Sermons with a variety of ideas and doctrine ring in churches and assemblies. However, the views and doctrine revealed through Joseph Smith Jr. on the atoning sacrifice and Resurrection of Jesus Christ were, and still are, distinct in many ways.

Joseph Smith proclaimed that he knew the resurrected Savior. He declared that in 1820, as a teenage boy, he saw God the Father and Jesus Christ in a grove of trees near his home in New York. At that time, the Savior instructed him about the churches of his day as well as "many other things" (Joseph Smith—History 1:20). Joseph Smith did not record all that the Savior taught him, but the pattern of receiving continuous revelation directly from the Savior remained throughout his life.

The Lord revealed many truths and commandments through Joseph Smith on many different subjects. The gospel revealed through the young Prophet was fundamentally different from any other theology. In fact, according to Joseph Smith, it would "revolutionize the whole world."[1] Joseph Smith also taught that "The fundamental principles of our religion are the testimony of the Apostles and Prophets, concerning Jesus Christ, that He died, was buried, and rose again the third day, and ascended into heaven; and all other things which pertain to our religion are only appendages to it."[2] Regarding the Atonement, the Lord revealed many revolutionary doctrines through Joseph Smith. Some examples of these doctrines are that Adam and Eve were forgiven for the Fall, that all the prophets from Adam to today knew and testified of the Atonement, that the Atonement works retroactively as well as proactively, details and insights into the two separate resurrections, that the great majority of mankind will inherit a degree of glory in the afterlife, and that Jesus Christ atoned for the sins of others on other worlds.

During a general conference of the church held in April 2005, Richard C. Edgley, first counselor in the presiding bishopric, testified of the power of the doctrines of the Atonement that were revealed through Joseph Smith:

> *Because of the Prophet Joseph Smith I understand more fully the magnitude of Christ's Atonement. Because of the Prophet Joseph, I better understand the significance of the Garden of Gethsemane—a place of great suffering as Christ assumed our personal suffering not only for our sins, but also for our pains, infirmities, trials, and tragedies. I understand the infinite and eternal nature of His great and last sacrifice. I better understand the love of our Savior exemplified in His last redeeming act. Because of Joseph Smith, my love and gratitude for the Savior is magnified and my worship more meaningful.*[3]

Despite the Prophet's emphasis on and the uniqueness of the doctrine of the Atonement, what was revealed through him is not widely known nor often discussed in the world. Bruce C. Hafen wrote,

> Sometimes we do not fully recognize the strength of the Church's position on the most crucial doctrines of Christianity . . . Yet the gospel's insights remain relatively hidden from a society that has been consciously and cleverly persuaded by the evil one that the church of the Restoration knows least—when in fact it knows most—about Jesus Christ's role as our personal Savior. The adversary has known exactly what he is doing. He has been engaged in one of history's greatest cover-ups. [4]

What Satan has worked so hard to cover up is worth trying to bring to further light.

A New View on Revelations about the Atonement

Though much of the world is naïve to Latter-day Saint doctrine on the Atonement, members of the Church in general are familiar with what the Lord revealed through Joseph Smith. However, these great revelations can be taken for granted. Our place in history gives us a great advantage that we sometimes ignore. We live in a day where the Church is the most popular it has ever been. It has millions of members in over a hundred countries and the current prophet is even interviewed on primetime television. Every person in a family can easily have a personal set of scriptures, which include revelations received by Joseph Smith. Scholars publish volumes on the Prophet Joseph Smith and what was revealed through him. There are gospel databases available making teachings and quotes just a matter of a few moments and a few mouse clicks away.

In contrast, imagine the beginning of March, 1830. The Church was not yet organized. The Book of Mormon would not become available until the end of the month. Joseph Smith had only received sixteen of the revelations that are now recorded in the Doctrine and Covenants. However, there was no Doctrine and Covenants yet, nor Pearl of Great Price. There were no apostles, seventies, mission presidents, or bishops. In fact, the Church would be organized a month later with only six members. There were no temples or meetinghouses. There were no Church manuals. As time continued and the Prophet received revelations, they were not necessarily readily available to the growing body of the Church. Some acquired their own handwritten copies. Many waited in eager anticipation for a compilation to be published.

The Lord gave the Prophet numerous revelations from 1828 to 1843, which are now found in the Doctrine and Covenants. Though Joseph Smith received these revelations over fifteen years, he received almost half of them in just two years, from March 1830 to February 1832 (see D&C 1; 19–76; 133). Also during these two years, he made additions and changes to the Bible. These alterations were also revelation from the Lord. The Prophet began the work in 1830 and had completed the majority of corrections and additions by mid 1832.[5] In many cases, there were interesting themes and correlations between the revelations now recorded in the Doctrine and Covenants and the Joseph Smith Translation of the Bible (hereafter referred to as JST). This was a period of many and great revelations. Though these were the first two years of The Church of Jesus Christ of Latter-day Saints, the revelations during this time provide the majority of the unique doctrines regarding the Atonement and a strong doctrinal base for the future.

The Lord revealed at least eighty significant elements regarding the Atonement from March 1830 to February 1832. This book analyzes them chronologically, month by month. At the end of each month or group of months, a summary of what was revealed through the Prophet during that time period is provided. This approach makes it easier to understand what the Lord revealed through Joseph Smith, when He revealed it, and what had already been revealed concerning the "great and last sacrifice" of the Atonement of Jesus Christ (Alma 34:10).

Chapter 2

BACKGROUND INFORMATION

IT IS HELPFUL TO DISCUSS THREE ELEMENTS of Church history before continuing. They will give more depth to this study, and are often mentioned throughout this book. First, the Lord had already revealed many truths on the Atonement through the Book of Mormon and several revelations received in 1829. Second, the Prophet attempted to print a collection of the revelations we will analyze in what was called the Book of Commandments. Later, the Church successfully published these revelations in several editions of the Doctrine and Covenants. And finally, the Lord commanded Joseph Smith to make corrections and additions to the entire Bible.

*R*evelations on the Atonement in 1829

Before analyzing what was revealed on the Atonement through Joseph Smith from 1830–1832, it is important to note that the Lord had already revealed much on the subject in the previous years. Joseph Smith received sixteen of the revelations now included in the Doctrine and Covenants in 1828 and 1829 (see D&C 3–18). Of these two years, 1829 produced the most significant insights on the Atonement.[6]

Also during this time, Joseph Smith translated the Book of Mormon. From 1827 to 1828, Joseph Smith translated 116 pages of the Book of Mormon with Martin Harris as scribe. Sadly, those pages, and the truths in them were lost.[7] Joseph Smith translated the majority of what is now the Book of Mormon from April to June 1829 with Oliver Cowdery as scribe.[8] It was first published and made available for purchase on March 26, 1830.[9] The Book of Mormon is so rich with commentary and insights about the Atonement of Jesus Christ that to discuss them would require another book. However, it seems necessary to briefly summarize some of its teachings to lay a useful doctrinal foundation for the revelations received between March 1830 and February 1832. Other doctrines in the Book of Mormon will be discussed later in this book.

The Atonement Satisfied the Demands of Justice

As was mentioned, Joseph Smith translated the great majority of the Book of Mormon from April to June of 1829. The Book of Mormon beautifully explains eternal reasons that Jesus Christ had to suffer in the Atonement. Justice demands certain consequences of sin; the Savior felt those consequences for every sin of all humanity. The Book of Mormon teaches that every sinner must feel guilt and remorse of conscience (see 2 Nephi 9:14–15; Enos 1:6; Mosiah 5:18; Alma 42:18). It also instructs that every sinner must be cut off from the presence of God (2 Nephi 1:20; 4:4; Alma 9:13–14; 36:30; 37:13; 38:1; 50:20; Helaman 12:21). All who ever sin would feel these consequences forever—if there were no Atonement. The Book of Mormon even states that sinners would become like the devil and his angels, hopeless spirits, if Jesus Christ had not sacrificed Himself for all mankind (see 2 Nephi 9:8–9). Thankfully, the Atonement satisfies these demands of justice and provides a way for mankind to repent and escape such consequences (see 2 Nephi 2:7; 9:26; Mosiah 2:38; Mosiah 3:25–27; Alma 42:16; Moroni 7:28). The Book of Mormon is perhaps the best place in scripture where it is taught that Jesus Christ suffered for all of mankind's sickness as well (see Alma 7:11).

All Mankind Will Resurrect because of the Atonement

The Book of Mormon also plainly teaches about the Resurrection. The word "resurrection" never appears in the Old Testament, but it was a much-discussed topic in the New Testament. Some biblical passages appear as though they teach that only some will resurrect. Daniel taught, "And *many* of them that sleep in the dust of the earth shall awake" (Daniel 12:2, italics added). John recorded the Savior's words, "the Son quickeneth *whom he will*" (John 5:21, italics added). Paul wrote, seemingly uncertain, "*If* by any means I *might* attain unto the resurrection of the dead" (Philippians 3:11, italics added). Paul also wrote, "but *if* the spirit of him that raised up Jesus from the dead dwell in you, he that raised up Christ from the dead shall also quicken your mortal bodies by his Spirit that dwelleth in you" (Romans 8:11, italics added). Other passages seem to teach that all will resurrect. John recorded that the Savior taught, "all that are in the graves . . . shall come forth" (John 5:28–29). Paul wrote to the Corinthians, "For as in Adam all die, even so in Christ shall all be made alive" (1 Corinthians 15:22). The Book of Mormon clarifies the doctrine of who will be resurrected. Amulek taught, "all shall rise from the dead" (Alma 11:41). Alma proclaimed, "All shall come forth from the dead . . . all shall rise from the dead" (Alma 40:4–5). Moroni taught, "all men shall be awakened by the power of God . . . all shall stand before his bar" (Mormon 9:13). Joseph Smith recorded further revelation that supported and built on this doctrine of universal resurrection over the next two years.

The Fall was Both Planned and Necessary

The Book of Mormon teaches clearly that Adam and Eve's Fall was planned and necessary. Nephi wrote, "All things have been done in the wisdom of him who knoweth all things. Adam fell that men might be; and men are, that they might have joy" (2 Nephi 2:24–25). Moroni wrote, "by Adam came the fall of man. And because of the fall of man came Jesus Christ . . . and because of Jesus Christ came the redemption of man" (Mormon 9:12). Joseph Smith revealed much on the doctrine of the Fall during the first two years of the organized Church.

The Atonement Is Infinite and Was Planned from the Foundation of the World

The Book of Mormon expands the comprehensible limits of the Savior's sacrifice. Nephi taught that "the atonement . . . is infinite" (2 Nephi

25:16). Amulek added that it had to be "infinite and eternal" to pay for every broken law (Alma 34:14). Book of Mormon prophets also testified that the Atonement, or "the redemption . . . was prepared from the foundation of the world" (Mosiah 15:19; see also 1 Nephi 10:18; Mosiah 17:13; Alma 12:30). The Atonement was planned from the beginning of the world and is infinite. The Lord also expanded on these doctrinal principles through revelation to Joseph Smith.

The Worth of Human Souls and the Atonement

In June of 1829, the Book of Mormon neared completion. Also in June, the Lord revealed through Joseph Smith a touching connection between human worth and Jesus Christ's sacrifice: "Remember the worth of souls is great in the sight of God; For, behold, the Lord your Redeemer suffered death in the flesh; wherefore he suffered the pain of all men, that all men might repent and come unto him. And he hath risen again from the dead, that he might bring all men unto him, on conditions of repentance" (D&C 18:10–12). According to the revelation, mankind is worth the suffering and death of Jesus Christ.

Joseph Smith recorded the Savior's description of His suffering as "the pain of all men" (D&C 18:11). This is an all-inclusive statement. There are no listed exceptions, no statements of only the righteous, or those of His time. He simply stated, "all men." The Lord also revealed that His motivation for performing the Atonement was that "all men might repent and come unto him." This is another all-inclusive statement. The Atonement is proof that the worth of souls is great in the Lord's eyes.[10]

REVELATIONS ABOUT THE ATONEMENT IN 1829

1. The Atonement satisfied the demands of justice.

2. All mankind will resurrect, the good and the evil, because of the Atonement.

3. The Fall of Adam and Eve was planned and necessary.

4. The Atonement is infinite and was planned from the foundation of the world.

5. Joseph Smith recorded that the Savior Himself taught that mankind was worth His suffering.

6. Jesus Christ suffered the pains of all mankind.

Joseph Smith continued to record numerous other insights concerning the Atonement over the next two years that not only built on the teachings of the Book of Mormon and the revelations received from 1828 through 1829 but also expanded the revealed knowledge of the Atonement, deepened its meaning, and presented enlightening doctrines that are essential for humanity.

The Book of Commandments and the Doctrine and Covenants

Before continuing, it will also be helpful to give a brief history of the compilations made that contained the Prophet's revelations, The Book of Commandments and the Doctrine and Covenants. The Book of Commandments was an early collection of revelations that was printed in 1833. By November 1, 1831, over sixty revelations had been recorded. Joseph Smith and other Church leaders collected these revelations, and compiled them for publication.[11] Many early Saints did not have access to the Prophet's revelations at this point. Joseph Smith called a special conference with the elders of the Church in Kirtland, Ohio, to discuss the details of publishing. During this conference, Joseph Smith received an inspired introduction to the book: "this is . . . my preface unto the book of my commandments, which I have given them to publish unto you, O inhabitants of the earth" (D&C 1:6). Also during this conference, Joseph Smith received another revelation in which the Lord declared His testimony of the revelations, "And now I, the Lord, give unto you a testimony of the truth of these commandments which are lying before you" (D&C 67:4). After much discussion, those at the conference decided to publish 10,000 copies of the presented revelations under the title "Book of Commandments."[12] Oliver Cowdery and John Whitmer would deliver a copy of the revelations for printing to W. W. Phelps, a publisher who had joined the Church in 1831, in Independence, Missouri.

W. W. Phelps printed sixty-five chapters of the revelations by July of 1833. Tragically, on July 1, 1833, mob violence destroyed the printing house, the press, and most of the copies of the book. Joseph Fielding Smith, great nephew of Joseph Smith, later wrote, "I only know of five or six copies that are to be found today." [13] Though many of the Saints never had the opportunity to have their own copy of the revelations until years later, the Book of Commandments was the first compilation of the Prophet's revelations that was approved by the Lord and the leadership of the Church for general publication. [14]

The same revelations included in the Book of Commandments as well as additional revelations were later compiled and printed under the name Doctrine and Covenants. The majority of the revelations from the Book of Commandments were left untouched when printed in the Doctrine and Covenants. However, there were several changes. Where there was a significant change in the text, this book quotes the original Book of Commandments. Where there were no significant changes, this book quotes the Doctrine and Covenants, because of its accessibility and its acceptance as canonized scripture.

The Doctrine and Covenants was a subsequent and more complete collection of revelations. In 1834, the First Presidency of the Church, which consisted of the Prophet and his two counselors, along with a few others, formed a committee to again attempt to publish the revelations. The compilation was approved in the conference of the Church on August 17, 1835. It had the title of Doctrine and Covenants, and included 102 sections. As time continued, the Prophet received more revelations. The Church printed subsequent editions in 1844, 1876, 1921, and 1981. Each edition printed more revelations than the previous. The Doctrine and Covenants quoted in this book refers to the most recent of these publications, in which there are 138 revelations recorded. All but seven of these came through the Prophet Joseph Smith.

The Joseph Smith Translation of the Bible

It would also be useful to review the history of the Joseph Smith Translation of the Bible (JST). The JST consists of corrections and additions Joseph Smith felt inspired to make to the King James Version (KJV) of the Bible. Joseph Smith began this translation of the Bible in June 1830. [15] He called this work a "branch of [his] calling." [16]

The Doctrine and Covenants shows that revelation directed the process of correcting and adding to the Bible. The Lord specified who should serve as Joseph Smith's scribes (see D&C 25:6; 35:20; 47:1). He told the Prophet when and where he should work on the translation (see D&C 37:1; 73:3). He instructed on several occasions for the Saints to build a house for printing the new translation (see D&C 41:7; 94:10; 104:58; 124:89).

Revelation also indicated where in the biblical text Joseph Smith should work. The Prophet had translated the opening chapters of Genesis when, on March 7, 1831, the Lord commanded him to stop translating the Old Testament and begin on the New (see D&C 45:60). According to the date on the translation manuscript of Matthew 1, the Prophet Joseph began his work on the New Testament the next day. [17] As he finished the New Testament and worked on the Old, the Lord continued to guide and inspire him. Revelation directed the Prophet not to translate the Apocrypha (see D&C 91:1–6). Joseph Smith finished his work through both the Old and New Testaments on February 2, 1833. [18]

Throughout his life, Joseph Smith taught about the need for the JST. He wrote on February 16, 1832, "From sundry revelations which had been received, it was apparent that many important points touching the salvation of man, had been taken from the Bible, or lost before it was compiled." [19] He also taught on October 15, 1843, "I believe the Bible as it read when it came from the pen of the original writers. Ignorant translators, careless transcribers, or designing and corrupt priests have committed many errors." [20] Earlier that same year he also commented, "There are many things in the Bible which do not, as they now stand, accord with the revelations of the Holy Ghost to me." [21] The JST identified and corrected many of these errors.

It is important to discuss an interesting command Joseph Smith received on February 9, 1831, regarding the JST: "Thou shalt ask, and my scriptures shall be given as I have appointed, and they shall be preserved in safety; and it is expedient that thou shouldst hold thy peace concerning them, and not teach them until ye have received them in full. And I give unto you a commandment that then ye shall teach them unto all men; for they shall be taught unto all nations, kindreds, tongues and people" (D&C 42:56–58). This revelation commanded the Prophet not to teach about his changes until the whole work was complete. Joseph Smith was obedient. Therefore, teachings in his personal sermons relating directly to principles in the translation would not appear until after July of 1833. Because of this, teachings after this date are consulted.

Revelation gave several reasons for the translation, but one is particularly pertinent to the Atonement. A revelation directed to Fredrick G. Williams through Joseph Smith declared, "Now my servant Joseph Smith, Jr. is called to do a great work and hath need that he may do the work of translation *for the salvation of souls.*" [22] Joseph Smith received a further statement reiterating this grand purpose of the JST: "and the scriptures shall be given, even as they are in mine own bosom, *to the salvation of mine elect*" (D&C 35:20; emphasis added). Nothing could be more relevant to salvation than the doctrine of the Atonement.

The JST can be studied in many different publications. The Community of Christ, formerly the Reorganized Church of Jesus Christ of Latter-day Saints, owns the copyright to the JST. They have added the changes to the text of the Bible and printed it under the name, *The Holy Scriptures.* Referencing this format can lead to a little confusion because there are some alterations in the numbering of chapters and verses between this printing and King James Version Bibles. In the Bible printed by The Church of Jesus Christ of Latter-day Saints, many of the JST changes are included in the footnotes corresponding to the verses altered. The additions the JST made to the beginning chapters of Genesis are included as the Book of Moses in the canonized Pearl of Great Price. Also, there are other published available compilations of JST changes showing what was changed and referenced by conventional biblical chapters and verses. [23] Another way to study the JST is through a newly printed form of the Prophet's original documents. [24] To facilitate referencing in this book, the JST changes that are included in the canonized Book of Moses, are referenced to the chapter and verse in Moses. Other JST changes are referenced by the letters JST and the chapter and verse in a conventional Bible, and can be found in the previously listed sources.

Chapter 3

REVELATIONS ABOUT THE
ATONEMENT IN 1830

IT HAD BEEN A DECADE SINCE JOSEPH SMITH saw God and Jesus Christ in the grove of trees outside his home in Palmyra, New York. The year was now 1830, and Joseph Smith was twenty-four years old. It was a monumental year in history for revelation on the Atonement. The Book of Mormon, translated by Joseph Smith, was first made available for purchase on March 26, 1830. It plainly and clearly revealed the teachings of ancient prophets about Jesus Christ's sacrifice. During 1830, the Lord revealed to Joseph Smith nineteen revelations that are now part of canonized scripture in the Doctrine and Covenants (see D&C 19–37). Joseph Smith also began his inspired work making corrections and additions to the Bible. This work contributed many new insights about the Atonement of Jesus Christ, and what ancient prophets understood about it.

arch 1830

Joseph Smith received in March the first revelation of 1830 that was included in the Book of Commandments, and later the Doctrine and Covenants. It is important to be familiar with the events of that month in order to understand the revelation; the printing of the Book of Mormon hung in the balance. E. B. Grandin, who had agreed to publish 5,000 copies of the book, feared he would never be paid for the work and that his business would be financially ruined. Martin Harris knew of the divine authenticity of the Book of Mormon and contracted to pay Grandin $3,000 for the job. He even mortgaged his farm as collateral. Martin Harris's wife was definitely opposed to such financial risk for what she thought was a questionable religious movement. With so much for Martin Harris to lose, he grew extremely anxious, and desperately wanted direction from the Lord. Joseph Smith recorded the Lord's response to Martin Harris. This revelation, found in D&C 19, included many eye-opening insights on the Atonement that cannot be found anywhere else in scripture. [25]

Jesus Christ Recounted His Sacrifice to Inspire the Sacrifice of Martin Harris

In this revelation, Jesus Christ disclosed the only recorded firsthand account of His suffering. The Savior described His own anguish as "suffering [which] caused myself, even God, the greatest of all, to tremble because of pain, and to bleed at every pore, and to suffer both body and spirit" (D&C 19:18).[26] Surely only the greatest of pain could make "the greatest of all" tremble and bleed. Such suffering is unfathomable to mortals. In fact, in the same revelation, the Lord told Martin Harris that the pain was incomprehensible, "how sore you know not, how exquisite you know not, yea, how hard to bear you know not" (D&C 19:15).

Though Martin Harris could not fully comprehend the Savior's suffering, the Lord recounted it with a calculated purpose. The Savior does not tell stories just to fill space or pass the time. After Jesus Christ gave such detail about His Atonement, He then told Harris to improve his prayers, to keep the commandments more diligently, and not to covet his own property but to "impart it freely to the printing of the Book of Mormon" (D&C 19:26). This last subject received special attention (see D&C 19:34–35). Why did the Lord first tell Harris a personal account of His suffering before commanding him to give of his money and property? Perhaps it put Harris's sacrifice in perspective. Perhaps understanding the Savior's sacrifice made it easier for Martin Harris to make sacrifices of his own.

Joseph Smith later taught the principle that mankind must be willing to sacrifice everything in order to be saved:

Let us here observe, that a religion that does not require the sac-rifice of all things never has power sufficient to produce the faith necessary unto life and salvation. . . . It was through this sacri-fice, and this only, that God has ordained that men should enjoy eternal life. . . . When a man has offered in sacrifice all that he has for the truth's sake, not even withholding his life, and believ-ing before God that he has been called to make this sacrifice because he seeks to do his will, he does know, most assuredly, that God does and will accept his sacrifice and offering, and that he has not, nor will not seek his face in vain. Under these circumstances, then, he can obtain the faith necessary for him to lay hold on eternal life. [27]

Joseph Smith recognized that God would ask for great sacrifices, and that humanity needs the faith to make them in order to be saved. This revelation taught Martin Harris to live this principle by sacrific-ing a portion of his property to pay for the printing of the Book of Mormon.

The Shedding of Blood in Gethsemane Was an Essential Part of the Atonement

As recorded by Joseph Smith, Jesus Christ's firsthand account of His sacrifice included the Redeemer's suffering in Gethsemane as part of His Atonement. No biblical passage does the same. Matthew, Mark, and Luke all dealt with the event relatively quickly, and John left it out entirely (see Matthew 27:37–45; Mark 14:32–42; Luke 22:39–46). Luke is the only Gospel that recorded the detail that Jesus Christ's "sweat was as it were great drops of blood falling down to the ground" (Luke 22:44). This biblical passage did not clarify whether Jesus Christ literally sweat blood, or if his sweat was metaphorically large drops of blood. The lack of detail has resulted in some confusion over the purpose and result of Jesus Christ's anguish in the garden. In Doctrine and Covenants nineteen, Jesus Christ clarified that He literally did "bleed at every pore," and that His blood dripped in atonement (D&C 19:18).

The JST also included this doctrine regarding the Savior's bleed-ing. Sometime between November of 1831 and February of 1832, the Lord inspired Joseph Smith to make a small change to Luke 22:44.

Instead of the wording, "and his sweat was as it were great drops of blood," the JST reads, "and he sweat as it were great drops of blood" (JST Luke 22:44). This simple modification changed the word "sweat" from a noun to a verb. During the Atonement, the liquid was not common sweat, but literal blood, which flowed from every pore. His garment would have been stained bright red in Gethsemane. [28]

Jesus Christ Suffered Both Physically and Spiritually in Gethsemane

Sweating blood exemplified Jesus Christ's great physical pain during the Atonement. However, that was not the only way He suffered. This revelation stated that the Savior suffered both physically and spiritually in Gethsemane, or "both body and spirit" (D&C 19:18). It also taught Martin Harris and Joseph Smith about Jesus Christ's spiritual suffering using their own personal experiences. The Lord stated, "in the smallest, yea, even in the least degree you have tasted [this suffering] at the time I withdrew my Spirit" (D&C 19:20). The revelation was probably referring to an incident that happened roughly two years before March of 1830. It was the loss of the 116 manuscript pages of the Book of Mormon. This tragedy resulted in great pain for both Joseph and Martin. In order to understand the Savior's comparison, a look into this history is helpful.

Joseph Smith's mother recorded that Martin Harris usually visited their home "in haste," but on the day he came to tell Joseph that he had lost the manuscript, he delayed for hours. He arrived, walking slowly. When he entered and was asked about the manuscript, "Martin pressed his hands upon his temples and cried out in a tone of anguish, 'Oh! I have lost my soul. I have lost my soul!'" [29] Lucy Mack Smith also recorded her son's reaction:

> He wept and groaned, walking the floor continually. . . . I
> besought him not to mourn so, for it might be that the Lord
> would forgive him, after a short season of humiliation and repen-
> tance on his part. But what could I say to comfort him when he
> saw all the family in the same state of mind that he was? Our
> sobs and groans and the most bitter lamentations filled the house.
> Joseph, in particular, was more distressed than the rest. . . . He
> continued walking backwards and forward, weeping and grieving

like a tender infant until about sunset, when we persuaded him to take a little nourishment. . . .

I well remember that day of darkness, both within and without. To us, at least, the heavens seemed clothed with blackness, and the earth shrouded with gloom. I have often said within myself that if a continual punishment, as severe as that which we experienced on that occasion, were to be inflicted upon the most wicked characters who ever stood upon the footstool of the Almighty—if even their punishment were no greater than that, I should feel to pity their condition. [30]

Such terrible pain was "the least degree" of Jesus Christ's spiritual suffering. Mankind's emotional trauma pales in comparison to the Savior's spiritual agony during the Atonement.

It is important to note that in the revelation's comparison between the suffering of Jesus Christ and that of Joseph Smith and Martin Harris, it defined spiritual suffering as a separation from God or His Spirit (see D&C 19:20). This is one place in scripture where it is inferred that the Savior's pain included moments where the Spirit withdrew from Him. This doctrine brings new light to Jesus Christ's cry on the cross, "My God, my God, why hast thou forsaken me?" (Matthew 27:46). At least during some portion of the Atonement, the Redeemer suffered alone, separated from the divine presence of His Father.

Jesus Christ's Atonement was an Act of Submission to the Will of the Father

This same revelation stated that by suffering spiritually and physically in atonement, Jesus Christ "accomplished and finished the will of . . . the Father" (D&C 19:2). Jesus practiced full submission to God. In fact, the Savior spoke of the Father as "him whose I am" (D&C 19:2). Along with this submissiveness, however, Joseph Smith recorded that Jesus Christ confessed, "[I] would that I might not drink the bitter cup, and shrink" (D&C 19:18). The Redeemer was personally reluctant to bear the full weight of the Atonement. The pain was so intense that it caused "the greatest of all, to tremble because of pain" (D&C 19:18). In such terrible anguish, He had a desire to "shrink" or recoil. This teaching is consistent with the Savior's attitude in Gethsemane recorded in the New Testament (see Matthew 26:42; Mark 14:36;

Luke 22:42). The Atonement is the only recorded instance when Jesus Christ expressed such a desire. Thankfully, Jesus Christ did not shrink, but bent His will to conform to His Father's desire saying, "Not my will, but thine, be done" (Luke 22:42).

In the fall of 1831, the Lord inspired Joseph Smith to make a change to the book of Matthew that also testified of Jesus Christ's submissiveness. He made an addition to the Savior's final recorded words on the cross, "it is finished" (John 19:30). The JST added that the Son of God told His father, "It is finished, thy will is done" (JST Matthew 27:50). These are Jesus Christ's final mortal words in the JST. They were to His Father, speaking nothing of the pain of the Atonement, but only of God's will. There was no selfishness in the Savior.

The Atoning Savior Subdued All Things to Himself

Doctrine and Covenants nineteen also explained the results of the Atonement of Jesus Christ. It taught that the Savior's sacrifice allowed Him to "subdue all things unto" Himself and retain "all power" (D&C 19:2–3).[31] In Noah Webster's 1828 Dictionary, a popular dictionary of Joseph Smith's day, the word "subdue" is defined, "To conquer by force or the exertion of superior power, and bring into permanent subjection; to reduce under dominion."[32] The great suffering of Jesus Christ allowed Him to conquer all of mankind's obstacles, and gave Him all the power necessary to save them.

The revelation boldly declared that Jesus Christ's power included the ability to destroy "Satan and his works at the end of the world" (D&C 19:3).[33] It is necessary to note that in order for Jesus Christ to "subdue" or bring Satan's power into subjection, He had to face it. This was not a radically different theological idea. John Wesley, a famous preacher to the layman in England in the 1700's whose teachings remained very influential in Joseph Smith's day, taught that in Gethsemane Jesus Christ was "grappling with the powers of darkness . . . surrounded with a mighty host of devils, who exercised all their force and malice to persecute and distract his wounded spirit."[34] Joseph Smith knew of Satan's great power on a personal level. He had previously faced it in the Sacred Grove. It nearly destroyed him. He wrote, "I was seized upon by some power which entirely overcame me, and had such an astonishing influence over me as to bind my tongue so that

I could not speak. Thick darkness gathered around me, and it seemed to me for a time as if I were doomed to sudden destruction . . . I was ready to sink into despair and abandon myself to destruction—not to an imaginary ruin, but to the power of some actual being from the unseen world, who had such marvelous power as I had never before felt in any being" (see Joseph Smith—History 1:15–16). God delivered Joseph Smith. As part of the Atonement, Jesus Christ faced the same evil being and triumphed.

Doctrine and Covenants nineteen not only testified of Jesus Christ's power over Satan, but that Satan's power was real. The devil is an elusive character through much of the KJV Bible. The word "Satan" makes its first biblical appearance in 1 Chronicles 21:10. "Lucifer" does not appear until Isaiah 14:12, which is also the only appearance of the word. The word "devil" is not in the Old Testament at all.[35] It first appears in Matthew 4:1.[36] His absence in scripture could lead to confusion about his reality and power. In the JST, however, Satan appears in the first chapter of the Bible, which will be discussed in more detail later. He tempted and challenged Moses. In this showdown, Moses cast Satan out in Jesus Christ's name (see Moses 1:21). In the JST, Satan is a real, dynamic character. He appeared in the first chapter and was overcome in the first chapter.

Jesus Christ's power over Satan is essential for humanity to return to God for according to the Book of Mormon, "if ye transgress the commandments of God . . . ye shall be delivered up unto Satan" (Alma 37:15). Without the Savior all mankind would be doomed to the devil's torment. Jesus Christ reclaims sinners from Satan's power. The JST added to John 14:30 that the Redeemer testified, "the prince of darkness . . . hath no power over me, but he hath power over you." Through the Atonement, man can overcome Satan as Moses did, as Joseph Smith did, and as Jesus Christ did.[37]

Jesus Christ Has Power to Judge because of the Atonement

It is readily apparent that Doctrine and Covenants nineteen is a revelation rich in new insights about the Atonement. Joseph Smith also recorded in this section that Jesus Christ retained "all power, even to . . . the last great day of judgment, which [He] shall pass upon the inhabitants thereof, judging every man according to his works and the deeds which he hath done" (D&C 19:3). The doctrine that Jesus Christ has the power to judge, and that He will, is also taught often in the Bible (see John 5:27; Acts 10:42; Romans 2:16; 14:10; 2 Corinthians 5:10).[38] The JST added to the Bible a bold and clear statement on the subject by Jesus Christ, "For the day soon cometh, that men shall come before me to judgment, to be judged according to their works" (JST Matthew 7:21). Doctrine and Covenants nineteen verified such scripture, and also made a clear connection between Jesus Christ's role as Judge and His role as Savior. The Atonement qualified the Savior to serve as judge.[39] Only the great Redeemer who paid for the sins of mankind and had "all power" could judge as to whether or not a person has repented and deserves exaltation.

The Atonement Allows Mankind to Choose Whether to Repent or Suffer

This revelation was expressly calculated to motivate Martin Harris and all mankind to repent. Joseph Smith recorded the Savior's declarations, "Every man must repent or suffer," and "I, God, have suffered these things for all, that they might not suffer if they would repent; but if they would not repent they must suffer even as I" (D&C 19:4; D&C 19:16–17). The revelation repeated this plea for repentance a total of eight times (see D&C 19:4, 13, 15–17, 20–21).

For those who repent, the Atonement spares them pain and suffering. However, there is a great responsibility with the availability of the Atonement. To those who refuse to repent, Joseph Smith recorded that the Savior declared, "they must suffer even as I" (D&C 19:17). This revelation boldly proclaimed mankind's two options.[40] God's children are responsible for their own sins, and if they do not utilize the Savior's suffering, they will have to suffer.

REVELATIONS ABOUT THE ATONEMENT MARCH 1830

1. Jesus Christ related a firsthand account of the Atonement from the Savior, which appears to be recounted to inspire Martin Harris to sacrifice his money to publish the Book of Mormon (in short, Jesus Christ's great sacrifice was a reality and should be remembered to inspire mankind to make necessary sacrifices).

2. Jesus Christ literally sweat blood in Atonement for all mankind.

3. Jesus Christ suffered both physically and spiritually in Gethsemane.

4. The Atonement was an act of submission to the will of the Father.

5. The atoning Savior subdued all things, including the power of the devil, to Himself.

6. Jesus Christ has the power to judge because of the Atonement.

7. The Atonement allows mankind to choose whether to repent or suffer.

pril 1830

On April 6, 1830, Joseph Smith organized The Church of Jesus Christ of Latter-day Saints. The entire membership of six people plus many onlookers took the sacrament on the occasion to remember the Lord's Atonement.[41] Joseph Smith received revelation that accompanied the organization that is now recorded as two different sections in the Doctrine and Covenants (see D&C 20–21).[42] This revelation, or series of revelations, differs from previous ones in its tone and audience. It was not intended for only an individual or a small group, but served as a document on ecclesiastical government for the Church then, and in the future. In fact, it came to be known among early Church members as the "Articles and Covenants of the Church." The teachings on the Atonement of Jesus Christ found therein serve as both a summary and a declaration of beliefs.

The Lord Revealed through Joseph Smith Foundational Beliefs about the Fall and the Atonement

This revelation outlined basic tenets of the Atonement. What is now Doctrine and Covenants twenty taught that God created men and women and gave them commandments (see D&C 20:18–19). However, because of transgression, "man became sensual and devilish, and became fallen man" (D&C 20:20). It is necessary to understand mankind's fallen condition to understand the Atonement of Jesus Christ. As was previously quoted, the Book of Mormon taught, "by Adam came the fall of man. And because of the fall of man came Jesus Christ . . . and because of Jesus Christ came the redemption of man" (Mormon 9:12). Because of Adam and Eve's transgression in the Garden of Eden, they were cast out from God's presence and became mortal. They could not return to God without a Savior. In this revelation's words, "by the transgression of these holy laws man . . . became fallen man" (D&C 20:20). Since that time, all humanity is born in a world away from God where death is inevitable. Without the Savior, to overcome sin and death, mankind would forever be fallen.

After explaining mankind's difficult state, the revelation continued, "Wherefore, the Almighty God gave his Only Begotten Son . . . He was crucified, died, and rose again the third day . . . That as many as would believe and be baptized in his holy name, and endure in faith to the end, should be saved" (D&C 20:21, 23, 25). This summary statement was doctrinally foundational to the new Church. The Father allowed His Son to be sacrificed to save His children from their fallen condition. Joseph Smith would record much more on the Fall in further revelation.

Joseph Smith Recorded Specific Instructions regarding the Administration of the Sacrament

The Atonement was also central to the Church in Jesus Christ's day. He taught His Apostles to remember His great sacrifice through the practice of the sacrament. According to revelation, the same Savior also guided the reinstatement of this ordinance in the nineteenth century. Joseph Smith recorded the following a few days before the Church was organized, "we were commanded to bless bread and break it with them, and to take wine, bless it, and drink it with them."[43] The revelation also instructed Apostles to "administer the flesh and blood of Christ according to the scriptures" (Book of Commandments 24:32).[44] This teaching emphasized the connection between the Atonement and the sacrament. It must have also turned Joseph Smith's attention to the New Testament accounts of the ordinance.

There are several New Testament texts that teach about the sacrament. The Gospels contain accounts of Jesus Christ Himself performing it. However, the Bible makes no mention of the words the Savior said to His Father to bless the sacrament, nor do they record Him distinguishing how often they should perform the ordinance.[45] The scriptures do record that the Savior's disciples continued to practice the sacrament after His death (see Acts 2:42, 1 Corinthians 11:26, 29). The Book of Mormon includes more detailed teaching about the sacrament. It testifies that Jesus Christ began the practice in the Americas (see 3 Nephi 18) and that He performed it often (see 3 Nephi 26:13). He ordained an apostle to have the authority to also perform the ordinance, and commanded the people to observe the practice "always" (see 3 Nephi 18:5; 18:12). The Savior specified that the sacrament be especially for "those who repent and are baptized" (3 Nephi 18:11). The Book of Mormon also includes the specific words to the prayer (see Moroni 3, 4). These scriptures show the pattern Joseph Smith was to follow.

With all of this scripture as a general doctrinal basis, the revelation in April of 1830 added some practical specifics. The Lord revealed through Joseph Smith the responsibilities of priests, teachers, and deacons regarding the sacrament, including repeating the specific words to the prayer (see D&C 20:46, 58, 76–79). They were the same words as those found in the Book of Mormon. The revelation related to any who wished to be baptized, that they needed to be taught sufficiently "all things concerning the church of Christ . . . previous to their partaking of the sacrament" and once they were baptized to "meet together oft to partake of bread and wine in the remembrance of the Lord Jesus" (D&C 20:68; D&C 20:75).

Revelations about the Atonement April 1830

1. The Lord revealed a foundational declaration regarding man's fallen condition and the Atonement.

2. The Lord instructed the Church to meet together often to partake of the sacrament to commemorate the Atonement, and indicated specific responsibilities of priests, teachers, and deacons regarding the sacrament. Those who wished to be baptized must first be instructed sufficiently about the gospel of Jesus Christ before partaking of the sacrament.

June 1830

June of 1830 brought more lessons on the Atonement. On June 9, thirty members and many other believers and investigators gathered for the second conference of The Church of Jesus Christ of Latter-day Saints. The ordinance of the sacrament was part of the gathering. Joseph Smith recorded about the experience, "many of our number prophesied, whilst others had the heavens opened to their view . . . Brother Newel Knight . . . saw heaven opened, and beheld the Lord Jesus Christ, seated at the right hand of the majesty on high." [46] Such a glorious and uplifting vision of the Redeemer at the beginning of June served as a supportive reminder for the end of the month. Joseph Smith was arrested on June 29. He recounted that while he was in custody, there "gathered in a number of men, who used every means to abuse, ridicule and insult me. They spit upon me, pointed their fingers at me, saying, 'Prophesy, prophesy!' and thus did they imitate those who crucified the Savior of mankind, not knowing what they did." [47] Not all of Joseph Smith's early lessons on the Atonement of Jesus Christ were words penned on paper. The Prophet's experiences contributed to his understanding and appreciation of the Savior. Also sometime in June, the Prophet began his work of making corrections and additions to the Bible. This work was the source of many insights and revelations on the Atonement.

Jesus Christ is the Only Begotten of the Father

In June, the Lord revealed through Joseph Smith a vision received centuries earlier by the Old Testament prophet Moses, one of the most notable prophets of the ancient world. [48] In the JST, this vision is the first chapter of the Bible. It is a touching encounter between Moses and God. Moses learned that he was literally a spirit son of God and that he was created "in the similitude of [God's] Only Begotten" (see Moses 1:4, 6, 7, 13; Moses 1:6). Moses is one son, in the image of another. However, clearly these brothers are not sons on the same level. The title "Only Begotten" separates and exalts Jesus Christ. His relationship to the Father is greater than Moses.'

Joseph Smith taught that Jesus Christ is "the Only Begotten of the Father according to the flesh." [49] Moses is a spirit child of God, but

Jesus Christ is both a spirit and a physical child of God. It is interesting that God taught Moses so definitively that Jesus Christ would be his "Only Begotten," for the Savior was not yet physically born. It must have been paramount to understand the Redeemer's relationship to the Father. In fact, the Book of Mormon teaches that Jesus Christ's divinity was necessary for Him to be able to endure the Atonement (see Mosiah 3:7; see also John 17:4–5).

The KJV Old Testament never refers to Jesus Christ as the "Only Begotten." The title first appears in John 1:14, and is used only six times (see John 1:14; 1:18; 3:16; 3:18; Hebrews 11:17; 1 John 4:9). The JST added the title, referring directly to the Savior, twenty-five times in the first eight chapters of the Old Testament (see Moses 1:6, 13, 16, 17, 19, 32, 33; 2:1, 26, 27; 3:18; 4:1, 3, 28; 5:7, 9, 57; 6:52, 57, 59, 62; 7:50, 59, 62).[50] Joseph Smith recorded it eleven times in the Doctrine and Covenants (see D&C 20:21; 29:42, 46; 49:5; 76:13, 23, 25, 35, 57; 93:11; 124:123).[51] Modern revelation made it clear that the Savior of the world was indeed the Only Begotten and literal Son of God in the flesh.

As God continued talking to Moses, He declared, "and mine Only Begotten is and shall be the Savior, for he is full of grace and truth" (Moses 1:6). God taught that Jesus Christ would be the Savior. In the five books of Moses in the KJV Bible, there are several prophecies of the Redeemer, however, they are somewhat cryptic, referring to the Savior as "Shiloh," "shepherd," "stone," "star," and "prophet" who would be raised up (see Genesis 49:10; 49:24; Numbers 24:17; Deuteronomy 18:15). In the JST, there is a clear proclamation that the Only Begotten would be the Savior beginning in the first six verses of the Bible. Moses, the great prophet who delivered the children of Israel, learned from God that Jesus Christ would come and atone for all mankind, making them truly free.

The Atonement
Transcends Time

As was previously mentioned, God said to Moses that Jesus Christ, the "Only Begotten is and shall be the Savior." This is a fascinating statement. Jesus Christ not only would be the Savior, but He was the Savior at the ancient time of Moses. In April of 1830, the Lord revealed that "as many as were before he [Jesus Christ] came in the flesh, from the beginning . . . as well as those who should come after" would be saved (Book of Commandments 24:18).[52] According to these teachings, Jesus Christ's saving power is not bound by time. It is retroactive as well as proactive. Though the Redeemer had not yet sacrificed Himself, ancient people at the time of this statement were utilizing the power of the future Atonement and were being saved.[53]

God knew the reality of the Atonement that was to come. He boldly stated, "But there is no God beside me, and all things are present with me, for I know them all" (Moses 1:6). This concept demonstrated God's omniscience. The Father had such faith and confidence in His Only Begotten, that He would atone for all of mankind, that the future event was a present reality with Him. And because it was a present reality with God, He allowed it to begin working even before it was accomplished.

This is a unique insight to the revelations and scripture brought through Joseph Smith. The Prophet had already translated the words of Book of Mormon prophets who testify of this truth over and over again. King Benjamin taught around 124 B.C., "whosoever should believe that Christ should come, the same might receive remission of their sins, and rejoice with exceedingly great joy, even as though he had already come among them" (Mosiah 3:13). Jarom wrote about 400 B.C. that his people were taught to "believe in him [Jesus Christ] . . . as though he already was" (Jarom 1:11). This may be quite an astounding concept to those who believe Christianity was not found on the earth until the time of Jesus Christ.

REVELATIONS ABOUT THE ATONEMENT
JUNE 1830

1. Moses testified that Jesus Christ is literally the Only Begotten Son of the Father in the flesh, an attribute necessary to complete the Atonement.

2. The Atonement of Jesus Christ transcends time, saving both those who lived before it occurred and those who would live afterwards.

$\mathscr{A}$ugust 1830

In August of 1830, Joseph Smith continued his work with the Bible. The Lord had specifically directed him the month before, "Let your time be devoted to the studying of the scriptures" (D&C 26:1). Joseph Smith also began to "arrange and copy" the revelations he had received. [54] This arrangement included the previously discussed truths about the Atonement found in the Doctrine and Covenants. Also in August, Newel Knight and his wife visited Joseph Smith. The Prophet found the sacrament appropriate for the gathering. He recorded, "In order to prepare for this I set out to procure some wine for the occasion, but had gone only a short distance when I was met by a heavenly messenger." [55] The angel's message is now recorded as Doctrine and Covenants twenty-seven and taught about the sacrament.

Remembering the Atonement is More Important than the Symbols of the Sacrament

The angel proclaimed to Joseph Smith that he spoke the words of "Jesus Christ, your Lord, your God, and your Redeemer" (D&C 27:1). He delivered the following message, "it mattereth not what ye shall eat or what ye shall drink when ye partake of the sacrament, if it so be that ye do it with an eye single to my glory—remembering unto the Father my body which was laid down for you, and my blood which was shed for the remission of your sins" (D&C 27:2). All scriptural accounts refer only to the use bread and wine. Such is also the case with the revelations found in the Doctrine and Covenants. This was a significant change. According to this revelation, remembering the Atonement is much more important than the symbols of bread, wine, or any appropriate substitute. [56] This teaching led to the current practice of the Church of using bread and water to commemorate the Atonement.

REVELATIONS ABOUT THE ATONEMENT AUGUST 1830

1. Substitutions for bread and wine may be made in the sacrament, when necessity dictates.

2. Remembering the Atonement is more important than the symbols used in the sacrament.

*S*eptember–*O*ctober 1830

By September 1830, Joseph Smith had been making corrections and additions to the Bible for three or four months. Although he did not record the exact dates for all of his work, he did record that he received the first chapter of Moses in June of 1830, and he received what is now Moses 2–5:43 sometime between June and October 21, 1830.[57] This means that Joseph Smith translated four biblical chapters over four to five months. If the Prophet's work was regular and consistent, he probably translated chapters four and five of Moses in the second half of this period. This rationale dates this work around September to October of 1830. Also, the Church held a conference beginning on September 26. In anticipation of the event, Joseph Smith received what is now Doctrine and Covenants twenty-nine. It is significant that this revelation testified of many of the same truths regarding the Atonement that Joseph Smith recorded in the JST in the same time period.

Satan Rebelled against Jesus Christ and the Atonement

As Joseph Smith continued his work on the Bible, the Lord revealed that Satan had a history of jealousy of the Savior. The first chapter of Moses had already intimated this idea. When Moses refused to worship Satan, the devil "threw a tantrum." He "ranted upon the earth, and commanded, saying: I am the Only Begotten, worship me" (Moses 1:19). That is quite a reaction. He was intensely jealous of Jesus Christ. Why? Surely the Savior and Satan met before Jesus Christ's mortal life. Lucifer's envy began before his encounter with Moses, before the Fall of Adam and Eve. The Lord revealed through Joseph Smith in September, that it began in "the beginning" (Moses 4:1). In fact, it is the story that led a soul to become the devil (see Moses 4:4). The great conflict in this tragedy deals with the Atonement.

Little is revealed in the Bible about the beginnings of Satan. Isaiah taught that the devil was "fallen from heaven" and that he wanted to "be like the most High" (Isaiah 14:12, 14). John the Revelator told of a war in which Satan and his angels lost, where they were "cast out" (Revelation 14:9). The JST rendition of Genesis added great insight to the premortal drama. The JST revealed that Lucifer became Satan. The future devil and God had a conversation. In this discussion, Satan had a proposition, "Behold, here am I, send me, I will be thy son, and I will redeem all mankind, that one soul shall not be lost, and surely I will do it; wherefore give me thine honor" (Moses 4:1). The devil wanted to be the Redeemer. He wanted to save every soul. However, with his apparent noble intentions, he also wanted God's honor and power. Initial reaction to this story seems to downplay the role of a Savior. It appears to be a calling, a job opening, or opportunity just waiting for ambitious or qualified individuals. As the revelation continued the role of Savior became even more profound and timeless.

Parenthetically, it is interesting to note that Satan appeared to use the term "thy son" synonymously with the Redeemer. One doesn't normally propose to be another's son. It is not usually a matter of choice. Yet, this event occurred before the account of Adam and Eve. It was before the creation of man. It appears as though Satan proposed to be born the literal Son of God on earth, to be as Jesus is.

God described Jesus Christ as "my Beloved Son, which was my Beloved and Chosen from the beginning" (Moses 4:2). The words "beloved" and "chosen" both intimate that Jesus Christ was special, set apart, and divine, even before this event, even before there was a Satan.[58] The word "chosen" undoubtedly has reference to Jesus' role of Savior. What greater role was He chosen for? Perhaps the scripture indicates that Jesus Christ had already been selected premortally to be Redeemer. It was not an opportunity for which anyone could apply. Jesus Christ said to His Father, "Thy will be done, and the glory be thine forever" (Moses 4:2). Jesus did not campaign to be Savior. It was not a goal or ambition. The Father chose Him to save the rest of His children. Jesus Christ agreed to do whatever the Father asked, and to glorify Him.

This JST chapter includes no definitive pronouncement of who would be the Savior. However, in the next verse, God termed Satan's proposal to be the Redeemer as rebellion. He proclaimed that Satan wanted to destroy the agency that God had given to man and wanted the power of God (see Moses 4:3). This proclamation indicates that God had a plan. He had established agency for His children, and He would have Jesus Christ as the Redeemer. Satan rebelled against that plan, against God's will, so as the Lord recounted, "By the power of mine Only Begotten, I caused that he should be cast down; And he became Satan, yea, even the devil, the father of all lies, to deceive and to blind men, and to lead them captive at his will, even as many as would not hearken unto my voice" (Moses 4:3–4). Even premortally, Jesus Christ had power over Satan. This incident has two very different endings for two of its main characters. One soul was thrust from God's presence to become the adversary of humanity. The other would be the Savior of the world. The essential difference was their attitude towards the Father and His plan to redeem His children.

The doctrine of a premortal life is new to many. It was also new to some in the Church. Orson Pratt taught, "Joseph Smith, a man of no education or learning, comparatively speaking, was commanded to translate the Bible by inspiration . . . This same doctrine [of the premortal life] is inculcated in some small degree in the Book of Mormon. However, I do not think that I should have ever discerned it in that book had it not been for the new translation of the Scriptures." [59]

It is interesting to note that the Lord confirmed the truthfulness of the premortal confrontation in the Doctrine and Covenants close to the same time as these JST changes. The revelation taught, "the devil was before Adam" (D&C 29:36), or Satan existed before the first couple came to earth. And before Adam and Eve there was a major event, "For he [Satan] rebelled against me [God], saying, Give me thine honor, which is my power; and also a third part of the hosts of heaven turned he away from me because of their agency" (D&C 29:36). This revelation added that the "honor" Satan wanted was God's power.

Two years later, Joseph Smith and Sidney Rigdon had a vision of the premortal drama, including Satan's fall. Joseph Smith's record of this vision taught that Satan was "an angel of God who was in authority in the presence of God" when he rebelled (D&C 76:25).[60] It was no wonder that "the heavens wept over him" (D&C 76:26), for he had been trusted. He was a leader until he openly rebelled against Christ, God, and the Atonement.[61]

The Fall Included
Spiritual Death

After the premortal drama, the JST includes the account of Adam and Eve. The same Satan who was cast out of God's presence "sought to destroy the world" (Moses 4:6). He tempted Eve to partake of the forbidden fruit, and Adam followed. This decision had harsh consequences.

As the Bible also testifies, they would have to work the earth for their food and Eve would suffer in childbirth labor. However, these were not the worst consequences. The Lord drove them out His presence and out of the garden. Imagine the guilt, the sorrow. Degraded from souls in God's presence to common laborers who would die in a harsh new world. God still spoke to them, but as the JST added, "and they saw him not; for they were shut out from his presence" (Moses 5:4). This teaching intimates that while they were in the garden they did see Him. They were literally in His presence, but as part of their consequences, that closeness to God ended.

In the Doctrine and Covenants, the Lord stated about the same time as these JST additions, "The devil tempted Adam, and he partook of the forbidden fruit and transgressed the commandment, wherein he became subject to the will of the devil" (D&C 29:40). It is no wonder this event is called the Fall. Adam and Eve fell from the Lord's presence and influence, into a temporal, fallen world where they were subject to Satan's influence. The devil had tempted them in the Garden, but they were not subject to his will until they had transgressed the commandment God had given them. The revelation also taught that Adam and Eve's fall was identified as spiritual death (see D&C 29:41). It declared that the wicked at the last day will experience the same tragic separation from God (see D&C 29:41). In other words, humanity today is still in danger of being subjected to the will of the devil and feeling the agony Adam and Eve experienced.

Animal Sacrifice Was a Type and Shadow of the Atonement

As Joseph Smith continued the translation of the story of Adam and Eve, the Lord inspired him to add the first clear biblical reference to the ancient practice of animal sacrifice. In the JST, the Lord commanded Adam and Eve "that they should worship the Lord their God, and should offer the firstlings of their flocks, for an offering unto the Lord" (Moses 5:5). Adam was obedient, but after many days, an angel visited and asked him why he offered sacrifices. "Adam said unto him: I know not, save the Lord commanded me" (Moses 5:6). The angel's answer in the JST plainly teaches what Old Testament readers are left to assume; "This thing is a similitude of the sacrifice of the Only Begotten of the Father, which is full of grace and truth" (Moses 5:7).

According to the JST, the very first man and woman knew that there was an Only Begotten of the Father, and that He would be sacrificed. This teaching is groundbreaking to many in the Christian world. The doctrine of the Atonement is not a two-thousand-year-old idea. It did not originate with the New Testament. It did not begin with the law given to Moses at Sinai. It was taught to the first man and woman on the earth from the very beginning of human history.

This addition to the Bible sheds light on the story of Cain's rejected sacrifice. The biblical beginning of Cain's decadence was a sacrifice he offered to the Lord. He offered "the fruit of the ground" while Abel brought "the firstlings of his flock" (Genesis 4:3–4). The Lord accepted Abel's sacrifice, but not Cain's. In the KJV, it appears as though God played favorites. Utilizing the JST, greater understanding emerges. God had commanded Adam and Eve specifically to sacrifice "the firstlings of their flocks" as a symbol of Jesus Christ's death (Moses 5:5). The Lord did not mention fruits. [62] Cain improvised on the Lord's commandments. He did things on his terms. It is no wonder that the Lord did not accept his sacrifice. The Prophet Joseph Smith later taught,

> By faith in this atonement or plan of redemption, Abel offered to God a sacrifice that was accepted, which was the firstlings of the flock. Cain offered of the fruit of the ground, and was not accepted, because he could not do it in faith, he could have no faith, or could not exercise faith contrary to the plan of heaven. It must be shedding the blood of the Only Begotten to atone for man; for this was the plan of redemption; and without the shedding of blood was no remission; and as the sacrifice was instituted for a type, by which man was to discern the great Sacrifice which God had prepared; to offer a sacrifice contrary to that, no faith could be exercised, because redemption was not purchased in that way, nor the power of atonement instituted after that order; consequently Cain could have no faith; and whatsoever is not of faith, is sin. [63]

Adam and Eve Were
Forgiven For the Fall

Through Joseph Smith, the Lord's teachings on Adam and Eve are forgiving and optimistic. This was not the case of other influential spiritual teachers of the Prophet's time. Reverend George Whitefield[64] spoke the following of Eve, "It is dreadful when those, who should be helpmates for each other in the great work of their salvation, are only promoters of each others damnation: but this it is."[65] He declared that Adam "proved false."[66] He also interpreted scripture to have taught, "Man was made in honor, God made him upright . . . But man so soon fell, and became like the beasts that perish, nay, like the devil himself, that it is scarce worth mentioning."[67] Alexander Campbell[68] used similarly harsh language. He taught that Eve

> stood attired in all charms of intellectual grandeur, moral beauty and ecstatic bliss. But in an evil hour she hearkened to the deceitful eloquence of Satanic flattery, and touched the alluring fruit of the one only forbidden tree. . . . In this eclipse of reason, in this aberration of heart, the sting of sin transfused its poison through her whole personality,—body, soul and spirit; and instantly the light of joy, and peace, and love, that beamed from her spirit-stirring soul-subduing eyes, vanished, a cloud of pensiveness sat brooding over her fallen countenance, and, handing the fruit to her admiring husband, he, in the blindness of his devotion to her charms, fascinated and overpowered by her former loveliness, thoughtlessly and recklessly, without a single remonstrance or demure, snatched it, ate it; in consequence of which, all his glory and dignity in a moment vanished away.[69]

John Wesley[70] taught that Adam "could not but know . . . that his disobedience would be fatal to all his seed. And if so, it was certainly both the greatest treachery and the greatest cruelty that ever was."[71]

In contrast, John Wesley also saw the Fall through a perspective of hope and optimism:

> We may gain infinitely more than we have lost. We may now attain both higher degrees of holiness, and higher degrees of glory, than it would have been possible for us to attain. If Adam had not sinned, the Son of God had not died: Consequently that amazing instance of the love of God to man had never existed, which has, in all ages, excited the highest joy, and love, and gratitude from his children.[72]

However, Wesley did not mention the possibility of Adam and Eve's forgiveness.

In the JST, following the explanation of why Adam and Eve performed sacrifices, the angel taught what must have been the most comforting doctrine possible for the fallen couple, "And thou shalt repent, and call upon God, in the name of the Son for evermore" (Moses 5:8). Repent? Adam and Eve could repent? The Bible mentions the many harsh consequences of the Fall, but does not teach that Adam and Eve could repent and be forgiven. The JST adds,

> And in that day the Holy Ghost fell upon Adam, which beareth
> record of the Father and Son, saying: I am the Only Begotten
> of the Father from the beginning, henceforth and forever, that as
> thou has fallen thou mayest be redeemed, and all mankind, even
> as many as will. (Moses 5:9)

The Holy Ghost confirmed the angel's words. Adam and Eve through the Atonement could return to the presence of God. Not only them, but all mankind—"as many as will." This is an enlightening doctrine. Instead of Adam and Eve being the first great tragedies in scripture, they become people of hope.

Adam praised the Lord and testified, "because of my transgression my eyes are opened, and in this life I shall have joy, and again in the flesh I shall see God" (Moses 5:10). Eve testified that she knew "the joy of . . . redemption" and that she and the obedient could have "eternal life" (Moses 5:11). Adam and Eve knew they could repent and return to God.

The Legacy of Calling
To Repentance

Reverend George Whitefield taught, "It is wonderful to observe, how gradually God revealed his Son to mankind."[73] Whitefield taught that God gave the promise of enmity between Eve's seed and Satan in Genesis 3:15, "and this the elect lived upon till the time of Abraham."[74] Joseph Smith recorded a vastly different situation for the first parents. They were not merely remembering one promise. As has been discussed, according to the JST, Adam and Eve knew from an angel of the Atonement. Then, as two comforted and inspired souls, they taught their children of the Savior, repentance, redemption, and eternal life (see Moses 5:12). In the JST, Moses recorded, "And thus the Gospel began to be preached, from the beginning" (Moses 5:58). "And Adam hearkened unto the voice of God, and called upon his sons to repent" (Moses 6:1).[75] Adam and Eve had the same gospel that was had in other time periods. It has been on the earth since the beginning.

A revelation Joseph Smith received in the same time period that he made these biblical changes taught, "I, the Lord God, gave unto Adam and unto his seed, that they should not die . . . until I, the Lord God, should send forth angels to declare unto them repentance and redemption, through faith on the name of mine Only Begotten Son. And thus did I, the Lord God, appoint unto man the days of his probation—that by his natural death he might be raised in immortality unto eternal life, even as many as would believe (D&C 29:42–43).

The Lord granted Adam and Eve time and opportunity to repent. Joseph Smith later taught, "Some say the kingdom of God was not set up on the earth until the day of Pentecost. . . . But I say, in the name of the Lord, that the kingdom of God was set up on the earth from the days of Adam."[76] In the JST, the Lord also gave Cain the chance to repent after his sacrifice, though he was on the verge of perdition (see Moses 5:25).

Doctrine and Covenants twenty-nine and the JST teach that there is an important connection between repentance and the cleansing power of the Atonement. The JST adds that as time passed, "The Lord God called upon men by the Holy Ghost everywhere and commanded them that they should repent; and as many as believed in the Son, and repented of their sins, should be saved" (Moses 5:14–15). It was an organized effort to help humanity repent and gain the blessings of the Atonement.

The Lord also instructed that there was a responsibility to repent or the Atonement will not and, moreover, cannot cleanse man. The ancient Saints taught, "as many as believed not and repented not, should be damned" (Moses 5:15). Doctrine and Covenants twenty-nine emphasizes the consequences of the "wicked" or "they [who] will not repent": "for behold, my blood shall not cleanse them if they hear me not" (D&C 29:17). It continues to teach, "And they that believe not . . . [will receive] eternal damnation; for they cannot be redeemed from their spiritual fall, because they repent not" (D&C 29:44). Without repentance, all remain stained by their sins.

All Mankind Will Be Resurrected
before the End of the World

Previous to September 26, 1830, the Doctrine and Covenants made several references to the Resurrection of Jesus Christ.[77] However, in Doctrine and Covenants twenty-nine, the Lord specifically spoke of His Second Coming, and of the effect of His Resurrection on others, "But, behold, verily I say unto you, before the earth shall pass away . . . shall all the dead awake, for their graves shall be opened, and they shall come forth—yea, even all" (D&C 29:26). The Lord taught and emphasized that "all" would resurrect. This confirms the teachings of Book of Mormon prophets. It also, however, teaches the doctrine that the resurrection will happen before the destruction of the world.

REVELATIONS ABOUT THE ATONEMENT SEPTEMBER–OCTOBER 1830

1. Satan rebelled against the Atonement premortally, wanting to be the Savior himself, which caused him to be cast out of God's presence.

2. The Fall included spiritual death.

3. Animal sacrifice was a type and shadow of the Atonement.

4. Adam and Eve were forgiven for the Fall.

5. From Adam on, messengers taught mankind to utilize the Atonement through repentance.

6. All mankind will resurrect before the end of the world.

November 1830

Joseph Smith wrote, "in the forepart of November [1830], Orson Pratt, a young man nineteen years of age, who had been baptized at the first preaching of his brother, Parley P. Pratt, September 19th (his birthday), about six weeks previous, in Canaan, New York, came to inquire of the Lord what his duty was, and received the following answer."[78]

The revelation is now recorded as Doctrine and Covenants thirty-four and included a powerful insight on the Atonement. Joseph Smith also continued his work with the Bible, which supplied more insights on the Redeemer's sacrifice.

The Savior Personally Declared That He So Loved the World That He Gave His Own Life

The Bible contains the Savior's words to Nicodemus, "God so loved the world that He gave his only begotten Son that whosoever believeth in him should not perish but have everlasting life" (John 3:16). This verse teaches of God's motivation for sending His Son. Doctrine and Covenants thirty-four taught of Jesus Christ's motivation to complete the Atonement. On November 4, 1830, Joseph Smith recorded a proclamation from "the Lord God . . . even Jesus Christ your Redeemer" (D&C 34:1). This revelation testified that the Savior "so loved the world that he gave his own life" (D&C 34:3). Previously, the Doctrine and Covenants revealed that Jesus Christ atoned to enable repentance and to accomplish the will of His Father (see D&C 18:10–12; D&C 19:16–17; D&C 19:2). Now, it added that love was His motivation as it was the Father's. The message is that the Father and the Son were united, not only in purpose, but also in feeling and motivation. Joseph Smith later wrote that Jesus Christ came to earth to "bear away sin as a mission of love."[79]

Through the Atonement, Mankind Can Become the Children of Jesus Christ

The Savior's loving Atonement allows mankind to become His sons and daughters. When God's children are baptized and enter into a covenant, they are born again. With every birth, a child gains a new parent. Joseph Smith had already translated King Benjamin's words in the Book of Mormon, which taught that those who make and keep their covenants are "children of Christ, his sons, and his daughters" (Mosiah 5:7). This birth, or covenant-keeping allows mankind to utilize the Atonement and gain all the eternal rewards the Redeemer provides. Joseph Smith had already recorded in May of 1829 the Lord's repetition of John 1:12 and its promise that He gives "power to become the sons of God" to all that receive Him (see D&C 11:30). These statements combine to teach that mankind can be born again through covenants, but that they also need power from the Lord. In other words, mankind cannot earn eternal life. Man has to qualify to receive "power" from Jesus Christ to obtain eternal life. The Savior changes the children of God. They don't change themselves alone.

As the revelation of November 1830 continues, the Lord testifies that He "gave his own life, that as many as would believe might become the sons of God. Wherefore [Orson Pratt] you are my son" (D&C 34:3). The Lord told Brother Pratt that he had been born again and blessed with the power to be a child of Christ.

One month later, in December, Joseph Smith recorded the Lord's words, "I am Jesus Christ, the Son of God, who was crucified for the sins of the world, even as many as will believe on my name, that they may become the sons of God, even one in me as I am one in the Father, as the Father is one in me, that we may be one" (D&C 35:2–3). The Lord taught that those who become God's sons are "one" with Jesus Christ and the Father. Therefore, those who truly become children of the Savior, may be saved through His Atonement. In the JST, after Adam made divine covenants, the Savior told him, "Behold, thou art one in me, a son of God; and thus may all become my sons" (Moses 6:68). Enoch also taught that "Many have believed and become the sons of God" (Moses 7:1). The Doctrine and Covenants repeats these truths many other times. [80]

Denying the Atonement Brings God's Wrath

Unfortunately, not all choose to qualify to become Jesus Christ's children. Joseph Smith continued his work on the Bible and the Lord added insights about Cain's posterity. The JST revealed God's intense feelings toward these people, "And God cursed the earth with a sore curse, and was angry with the wicked, with all the sons of men whom he had made" (Moses 5:56). The JST continued to explain why God was so upset, "For they would not hearken unto his voice, nor believe on his Only Begotten Son, even him whom he declared should come in the meridian of time, who was prepared from before the foundation of the world" (Moses 5:57). God obviously feels very passionately about His Son's sacrifice. Denying it brings His wrath.

The Savior Would be Born and Atone
In the Meridian of Time

In this same verse of the JST, God reveals that His Son would come "in the meridian [or middle] of time." This phrase is unique to the Doctrine and Covenants and the JST. [81] Though there are many biblical verses that prophesied of the Savior's coming, there were none that denoted the time until He was about to be born. [82] The first biblical indication of the time of Jesus Christ's birth was Gabriel's announcement to Mary. In contrast, the JST added that the Savior would be born in the meridian of time to the first generations on earth (see Moses 5:57). [83]

This phrase is also unique in its message. It was obviously not a detailed countdown to the Savior's birth. Those who believed and looked to Jesus Christ knew that He wouldn't come until the middle of time. They probably did not know when the end of time would be, so therefore, they would not be able to calculate the middle. However, they most likely deduced that Jesus Christ would not live mortally any time soon. Despite this knowledge, Adam and those who believed in the Savior knew that something yet to happen could save them.

REVELATIONS ABOUT THE ATONEMENT NOVEMBER 1830

1. Through revelation, the Savior stated that He so loved the world that He gave his own life.

2. Revelation included a further witness that through the Atonement, mankind can become Jesus Christ's children, and become one with Him.

3. Denying the Atonement brings God's wrath.

4. The Savior would be born and atone for all mankind in the meridian of time.

*D*ecember 1830

In December of 1830, Joseph Smith recorded what is now Doctrine and Covenants thirty-five through thirty-seven. These revelations testified of and directed the translation of the Bible (see D&C 35:18, 20; 37:1). One of these revelations included the previously discussed statement, "and the scriptures shall be given, even as they are in mine own bosom, to the salvation of mine own elect" (D&C 35:20). Fittingly, December was a historic month for JST insights on the Atonement. Joseph Smith wrote the following about this month:

> It may be well to observe here, that the Lord greatly encouraged and strengthened the faith of His little flock, . . . by giving some more extended information upon the Scriptures . . . a translation of which had already commenced. Much conjecture and conversation frequently occurred among the Saints, concerning the books mentioned, and referred to, in various places in the Old and New Testaments, which were now nowhere to be found. The common remark was, 'They are lost books;' but it seems the Apostolic Church had some of these writings, as Jude mentions or quotes the Prophecy of Enoch, the seventh from Adam. To the joy of the little flock, which in all, from Colesville to Canandaigua, New York, numbered about seventy members, did the Lord reveal the following doings of olden times, from the prophecy of Enoch. [84]

The account then shared the story of Enoch, which contains new insights into Jesus Christ's great sacrifice.

Enoch Preached a Very Instructive Sermon on the Fall and its Effects

Without the Joseph Smith changes, the Bible included little about the prophet Enoch. The book of Genesis teaches that Enoch was the son of Jared and Methuselah's father (see Genesis 5:18–21). It mentions that he "walked with god" when he was 365 years old, and then "he was not; for God took him" (Genesis 5:22, 24). The author of Hebrews testified that Enoch was translated and did not see death (see Hebrews 11:5). Jude quoted Enoch, saying that he prophesied of the Second Coming of Jesus Christ (see Jude 1:14–16). In short, the Bible mentions that Enoch lived, testified that the Savior would come again, and then was translated. [85] The JST adds considerable information about Enoch and his testimony of the Redeemer. According to the JST, Enoch heard a call from heaven commanding him to preach repentance (see Moses

6:27). The same voice testified about the people of the time, "And a hell I have prepared for them, if they repent not" (Moses 6:29). Enoch's divine mandate required him to teach his people how to repent and utilize the Atonement.

As has been mentioned, the Atonement gave humanity the ability to overcome the effects of the Fall. The Lord inspired Joseph Smith to add Enoch's intriguing sermon on the Fall to the Bible. This subject would have been very close to the hearts of Enoch's hearers because they knew Adam and Eve (see Moses 6:45). Enoch taught, "because that Adam fell, we are; and by his fall came death" (Moses 6:48). Though then men lived to be hundreds of years old, Enoch recalled that some ancestors had already died and said, "we are made partakers of misery and woe" (see Moses 6:45; Moses 6:48). The effects of the Fall were very real to Enoch's audience.

Enoch continued, "Satan hath come among the children of men, and tempteth them to worship him; and men have become carnal, sensual, and devilish, and are shut out from the presence of God" (Moses 6:49). Enoch described humanity's mortal state on earth as devilish and fallen from God. Mankind was not born that way, but each chose to become so when he or she sinned.

This revelation stands in stark contrast to much of the world's views on the Fall. Other influential religious thinkers of Joseph Smith's time had strong, contrasting feelings about human nature. Jonathan Edwards and George Whitefield were Calvinists and preached the total depravity of man. Edwards taught, "The inside of the body of man is full of filthiness, contains his bowels that are full of dung, which represents the corruption and filthiness that the heart of man is naturally full of."[86] Whitefield taught that humanity has an "in-being of sin," that man was "altogether conceived and born in sin," and that man "has no good thing in him by nature."[87] He also taught,

> *God would be just to damn [mankind] . . . just to cut him off, though he never had committed one actual sin in his life. Did ye ever feel and experience this any of you, to justify God in your damnation; to own that ye are by nature children of wrath, and that God may justly cut you off though ye never actually had offended him in all your life. . . . I am verily persuaded original sin is the greatest burden of a true convert. . . . We deserve to be damned ten thousand times over.*[88]

John Wesley taught his views on the subject while commenting on Seth's birth to Adam. He declared that Seth was born like his father, "sinful and defiled, frail and mortal, and miserable like himself. He was not only a man like himself, consisting of body and soul; but a sinner like himself, guilty and obnoxious, degenerate and corrupt. He was conceived and born 'in sin.'"[89]

Other religious thinkers were not as condemning of human nature. G. Frederick Wright summarized Charles Finney's views on the subject, "Finney insisted that, while we were not born with natures actually sinful, our natures were so constituted and circumstanced that sin was certain to be the universal characteristic of our first activities."[90] William Ellery Channing's rhetoric battled against the others. He taught that man was inherently good. He stated, "We believe that all virtue has its foundation in the moral nature of man."[91] Though opinions and teachings of the time varied, what Joseph Smith revealed was complex and unique.

According to the JST, though mankind is not born sinful, people fall into sin. Enoch boldly stated, "God hath made known unto our fathers that all men must repent" (Moses 6:50). The carnal, sensual, and devilish are not invited into God's presence. They must change.

Adam Utilized the Atonement Through Baptism

As part of Enoch's sermon, he quoted God teaching that all of mankind, not just Adam and Eve, were in His presence before their mortal births (see Moses 6:51). All humanity is in a fallen state. Enoch also taught how to repent and overcome the effects of the Fall. He relayed God's words,

> If thou wilt turn unto me, and hearken unto my voice, and believe, and repent of all thy transgressions, and be baptized, even in water, in the name of mine Only Begotten Son, who is full of grace and truth, which is Jesus Christ, the only name which shall be given under heaven, whereby salvation shall come unto the children of men, ye shall receive the gift of the Holy Ghost. (Moses 6:52)

It is significant that even anciently, humanity had to be baptized to overcome the Fall and receive salvation.

New Testament and Book of Mormon prophets alike taught the importance of baptism. It is the essential ordinance, which when coupled with repentance, washes away sins (see Mark 1:4; Acts 22:16; 2 Nephi 31:17; Moroni 8:11). Revelation urged Martin Harris back in March of this same year to "declare . . . faith on the Savior, and remission of sins by baptism" (D&C 19:31). Baptism is a funnel for the power of the Atonement, for surely no sins are washed away without it.

Later in his sermon, Enoch testified that Adam followed these steps by being baptized and receiving the Holy Ghost (see Moses 6:64–65). In the JST, the basic principles of repentance, the ordinances of baptism, and receiving the Holy Ghost date back to the first man. Interestingly, the word baptism is never mentioned, nor is the principle clearly taught in the Old Testament.[92] According to the JST, it was taught from the beginning. Some may find the doctrine that Adam was baptized difficult to believe, but Joseph Smith taught that from the beginning there were more ordinances essential for salvation than animal sacrifice:

> We all admit that the Gospel has ordinances, and if so, had it not always ordinances, and were not its ordinances always the same? Perhaps our friends will say that the Gospel and its ordinances were not known till the days of John, the son of Zacharias, in the days of Herod, the king of Judea. But we will here look at this point: For our own part we cannot believe that the ancients in all ages were so ignorant of the system of heaven as many suppose, since all that were ever saved, were saved through the power of this great plan of redemption, as much before the coming of Christ as since; if not, God has had different plans in operation (if we may so express it), to bring men back to dwell with Himself . . . and the ordinance or institution of offering blood in sacrifice, was only designed to be performed till Christ was offered up and shed His blood—as said before—that man might look forward in faith to that time . . . Our friends may say, perhaps, that there were never any ordinances except those of offering sacrifices before the coming of Christ, and that it could not be possible for the Gospel to have been administered while the law of sacrifices of blood was in force. But we will recollect that Abraham offered sacrifice, and notwithstanding this, had

*the Gospel preached to him. That the offering of sacrifice was
only to point the mind forward to Christ.* [93]

The most obvious ordinance during John the Baptist's time was baptism. However, authorized priesthood holders have always practiced the ordinances of the Gospel, and Adam was the first baptized.

Enoch recounted an instance where Adam asked the Lord why mankind must repent and be baptized. The Lord did not directly answer the question, but answered the unstated question that Adam sincerely and deeply wanted answered. Enoch recounted the Lord's response, "And the Lord said unto Adam: Behold, I have forgiven thee thy transgression in the Garden of Eden" (Moses 6:53). What powerful words! Previously in the JST, the Lord told Adam "and thou shalt repent," and "thou mayest be redeemed," but this was a proclamation from the Lord that Adam had been fully forgiven for the Fall (Moses 5:8–9). Through repentance and baptism, Adam was forgiven.

Reverend George Whitefield also taught that Adam and Eve "were saved." [94] However, he contended that though the first parents were tragically fallen, they simply held on to the promise that God would bruise Satan's heel through their seed and thus gained salvation. This is vastly different from the Adam and Eve who were forgiven and sought God with clean consciences revealed in the JST.

Children Are Redeemed from the Fall by the Atonement

In the JST, Enoch taught that Adam was and is not alone in his need to overcome his fallen nature. All mankind had a desperate need it could not meet on its own. Enoch taught that Adam and Eve's forgiveness was the source of "the saying abroad among the people, that the Son of God hath atoned for original guilt, wherein the sins of the parents cannot be answered upon the heads of the children, for they are whole from the foundation of the world" (Moses 6:54). Jesus Christ atoned for the original transgression. A newborn from Adam's day or today is not held responsible for the Fall. They are not carnal, sensual, and devilish when born. Because of the Savior, children are born "whole" or guiltless. Joseph Smith had already translated the Book of Mormon, which included King Benjamin's testimony that the Atonement covered children's sins (see Mosiah 3:16). However, Enoch's teaching significantly predates King Benjamin's. It goes back to the beginning.

Enoch's statement was a powerful commentary on how the Atonement satisfied original transgression. Interestingly however, in his sermon he continues to state a phrase that can be very confusing and even appear contradictory to his previous teaching. Enoch recounts that the Lord told Adam, "thy children are conceived in sin" (Moses 6:55). If they are not held responsible for the Fall, how are they "conceived in sin"? A quick look at a few previously stated principles clarifies the issue. God stated that He made "men before they were in the flesh" (Moses 6:51). Men existed before this life. The Lord also taught through Enoch that children "are whole from the foundation of the world" (Moses 6:54). Therefore, children were pure before they were born. They were pure in a previous state. Enoch made that clear. So if they are "conceived in sin," the change was not in them, but in their world or surroundings. The conception of children brings them from one place to another, and this world is a place of sin. Enoch referred to the fact that children would live in a world of sin. It was still true that "God hath atoned for original guilt" (Moses 6:54).

The context of the statement that children are conceived in sin is also very pertinent. In that same verse the Lord states, "even so when they begin to grow up, sin conceiveth in their hearts, and they taste the bitter" (Moses 6:55). As children grow, they feel the effects of the Fall. They begin to be tempted by Satan and sin. Enoch taught that all children need to overcome these effects. He preached, "Teach it unto your children, that all men, everywhere, must repent" (Moses 6:57).

Enoch's teaching intimated that little children would not need baptism until they grew older. Earlier in April of this same year, when the Church was organized, revelation put limitations on those who could join: "There cannot any one be received into this church of Christ, who has not arrived to the years of accountability before God, and is not capable of repentance" (Book of Commandments 24:50; see D&C 20:71). The Lord made no specification as to what age one reaches "the years of accountability," but His criteria for those who could be baptized excluded little children. In September of 1830, Joseph Smith recorded that, "little children are redeemed from the foundation of the world through mine Only Begotten" (D&C 29:46). This revelation also stated that little children "cannot sin" and that Satan cannot tempt children until they have become accountable (D&C 29:47).[95] These teachings clarify why little children do not need membership in the Church. This doctrine rejects the idea that original sin condemns unbaptized children to hell. Such children are salvationally safe and secure through the Atonement of Christ.

The JST also added to the Bible the doctrine that children are saved through the Atonement. On one occasion, Jesus Christ brought a little child before His Apostles, and said, "Whosoever therefore shall humble himself as this little child, the same is greatest in the kingdom of heaven" (Matthew 18:4). In the JST, Jesus Christ then made a doctrinal statement about children, "But these little ones have no need for repentance, and I will save them" (JST Matthew 18:11). In other words, disciples of the Savior must become like children because the Atonement has saved them. The Lord inspired Joseph Smith to clarify a similar issue in the next chapter. Jesus Christ's Apostles attempted to keep a group of children from meeting Him. This was not an episode of mean-spirited men oppressing children, rather, the Apostles wanted to deny the children access to the Savior simply because it would be spiritually inefficient use of the Savior's time. The disciples said, "There is no need [for the children to come to Christ], for Jesus hath said, Such shall be saved" (JST Matthew 19:13).

The doctrine that children are not held accountable for original transgression could be surprising to many. In fact, it would be to those in New Testament times. In January of 1832, Joseph Smith recorded that the Lord wanted "the tradition . . . done away, which saith that little children are unholy; for it was had among the Jews" (D&C 74:6). This revelation came in response to the Prophet's petition to the Lord for an explanation of 1 Corinthians 7:14. The revelation ended by saying, "Little children are holy, being sanctified through the atonement of Jesus Christ; and this is what the scriptures mean" (D&C 74:7).

Enoch Used the Symbols of Water, Spirit, and Blood to Teach about the Atonement

As Enoch continued his sermon, he repeated the necessity of repenting, being baptized, and receiving the Holy Ghost. He taught using the imagery of water, spirit, and blood. The world suffered the effects of the Fall, and all mankind entered into the world "by water, and blood, and the spirit" (Moses 6:59). Enoch used this imagery referring to the birth of any mortal. These same symbols show us how to utilize the Atonement. Speaking for the Lord, Enoch taught, "Inasmuch as ye were born into the world by water, and blood, and the spirit, which I have made, and so became of dust a living soul, even so ye must be born again into the kingdom of heaven, of water, and of the Spirit, and be cleansed by blood, even the blood of mine Only Begotten; that ye might be sanctified from all sin, and enjoy the words of eternal life in this world, and eternal life in the world to come, even immortal glory; for by the water ye keep the commandment; by the Spirit ye are justified, and by the blood ye are sanctified" (Moses 6:59–60; see also Moses 6:52).

There are many scriptural passages that discuss the necessity of being born again; however, none use all of the simple and compelling imagery of Enoch. Enoch's sermon summarized the Plan of God. Speaking for the Lord, he said, "This is the plan of salvation unto all men, through the blood of mine Only Begotten, who shall come in the meridian of time" (Moses 6:62).

The Atonement Empowered Jesus Christ to Be the Advocate of Mankind

In the JST, the ancient prophet Enoch continued to preach repentance (see Moses 7:10, 12). He even taught that if his audience did not repent, the Lord promised He would curse and kill them (see Moses 7:10). Unfortunately not everyone listened and the Lord revealed to Enoch the consequences. God himself would weep over them (see Moses 7:28). Enoch saw that the devil would laughingly veil the entire earth with darkness (see Moses 7:26). The Lord said, "these which thine eyes are upon shall perish in the floods; and behold, I will shut them up; a prison have I prepared for them" (Moses 7:38). The prison the Lord spoke of specifically referred to a spirit state after this life. The Lord, for good reason, called it a prison. There, they would not be free, but they would suffer in torment until Jesus came to earth and then returned to His Father, or in other words, until the Redeemer completed the Atonement (see Moses 7:39).

Though these souls would be rebellious and stubborn, according to the JST, God would not give up on them. They were not out of the Atonement's reach. The Lord spoke to Enoch, "And That [or Jesus Christ] which I have chosen hath pled before my face. Wherefore, he suffereth for their sins" (Moses 7:39). Jesus Christ pled before the Father for those unrepentant souls. He pled for those who "are without affection, and they hate their own blood" (Moses 7:33). He pled because "he suffereth for their sins."

Joseph Smith revealed that God continued to speak about those in prison, "inasmuch as they will repent in the day that my Chosen shall return unto me [they may be relieved of their agony], and until that day they shall be in torment" (Moses 7:39). Because of the Atonement, the spirits of Noah's time would not forever stay tormented in prison. Repentance was still possible for them, though Jesus Christ would not physically complete the Atonement until thousands of years later. Because of their sins they were denied the full, retroactive power of the Atonement: however, by virtue of a living Redeemer who pled for them, these sinners could ultimately be forgiven. It is worth noting that these verses do not mention that those killed in the Flood could gain eternal life with God, but that they could be forgiven.

In contrast to those who would not repent, many listened to Enoch, repented, and became part of one of the greatest spiritual success stories of all time. There was a great spiritual and physical polarization between those who repented and those who would not. Enoch saw that his people "in process of time [would be] taken up into heaven . . . even in the bosom of the Father, and of the Son of Man" (Moses 7:21, 24).[96]

At the beginning of the next month, on January 2, 1831, Joseph Smith recorded that the Redeemer pled for those who successfully followed Enoch. The revelation stated that the Lord indeed took the City of Enoch "into [His] own bosom" and that they were saved. The Lord continued, "I am Christ, and in mine own name, by the virtue of the blood which I have spilt, have I pleaded before the Father for them" (D&C 38:4). His sacrificial blood allowed Him to plead for Enoch's people. He pled for all, both those who would suffer in prison and those who would successfully return.

The concept of Jesus Christ pleading for mankind is not as clearly taught in the Old Testament outside of the JST. In the New Testament, Paul taught that Jesus Christ went to heaven "to appear in the presence of God for us" (Hebrews 9:24). John taught, "And if any man sin, we have an advocate with the Father, Jesus Christ the righteous" (1 John 2:1). Interestingly, the Lord provided through Joseph Smith a significant and clear reference to the Redeemer pleading by virtue of His blood, before His blood was spilt.

John provides the only time in the Bible that the word "advocate" appears (see 1 John 2:1), although the Doctrine and Covenants repeats the term many times. According to the 1828 Webster's Dictionary, the word advocate is derived from the Latin *advocatus*, which means "to call for or to plead for."[97] In September of 1830, Joseph Smith recorded the Lord's words; "Lift up your hearts and be glad, for I am in your midst, and am your advocate with the Father; and it is his good will to give you the kingdom" (D&C 29:5). The Lord repeated this reassurance to Ziba Peterson in October of 1830 (see D&C 32:3). Revelation testifies that Jesus Christ's pleading was not limited to ancient times.

In March of 1831, Joseph Smith recorded one of the Lord's strongest and clearest statements about his advocacy for mankind:

> *Listen to him who is the Advocate with the Father, who is pleading your case before him—Saying: Father, behold the sufferings and death of him who did no sin, in whom thou wast well pleased; behold the blood of thy Son which was shed, the blood of him whom thou gavest that thyself might be glorified; Wherefore, Father, spare these my brethren that believe on my name, that they may come unto me and have everlasting life.* (Book of Commandments 48:5–6; see D&C 45:3–5)

In this verse, there is no indication that Jesus Christ will attempt to excuse or rationalize any sin, but that by His merits, by His suffering, He will defend those that accept Him.[98] These verses give great comfort, for the Savior states that He is "pleading." This was not a one-time action, nor long past, but the very Savior who offered Himself as a sacrifice hundreds of years before, acted then and still acts today for the benefit of all mankind.

The Lord Revealed to Enoch That the Savior Would Come after the Flood and That He Saw Jesus Christ's Coming and Atonement

According to the JST, Enoch knew much about the Atonement. However, he didn't know every detail. He asked the Lord, "When shall the day of the Lord come? When shall the blood of the Righteous be shed, that all they that mourn may be sanctified and have eternal life?" (Moses 7:45). The Lord answered, "It shall be in the meridian of time, in the days of wickedness and vengeance" (Moses 7:46). It appears as though Enoch already knew this much, for he had previously declared twice that Christ would "come in the meridian of time" (Moses 5:57, 62). It is necessary to discuss the situation in which Enoch asked this question to gain further understanding. The Lord had just revealed to him that everyone, besides those on Noah's ark, would be destroyed. Enoch became bitterly depressed and refused to be comforted. "But the Lord said unto Enoch: Lift up your heart, and be glad; and look. And it came to pass that Enoch looked; and from Noah, he beheld all the families of the earth" (Moses 7:44–45). Life would go on. This vision was obviously not limited to Enoch's time. How many billions of families he must have seen. The Plan of Salvation would not be prematurely ended. With so many lives on the line, Enoch's question could have been more motivated by emotion rather than a need for information. Either he desired to know more specifically when Jesus Christ would come, or he wanted assurance for the other souls he saw.

Enoch already knew that Jesus Christ would come in the meridian of time, but when He heard the Lord's answer, his "soul rejoiced" (Moses 7:47). Then Enoch saw Jesus Christ's coming. He saw the Savior die and he joyously proclaimed, "through faith I am in the bosom of the Father, and behold, Zion is with me" (Moses 7:47). Enoch knew for certain that the Atonement would happen, even though he probably did not know exactly when.

The Lord Revealed to Enoch That the Savior Would Come through His Lineage

The prophecy of the impending Flood would directly affect Enoch's family. Though he would be translated, Noah, Enoch's great grandson, would live through the Flood. According to the JST, Enoch pled for his future family and the Lord covenanted that there would only be one Flood and "that a remnant of his seed should always be found among all nations, while the earth should stand" (Moses 7:52). This would be Enoch's seed, because the Lord "truly covenanted with Enoch that Noah should be of the fruit of his loins" (Moses 8:2). This seed was both Noah's and Enoch's posterity. "And the Lord said; Blessed is he through whose seed Messiah shall come" (Moses 7:53). Joseph Smith recorded that the Lord told Enoch that the Savior would come through his lineage. This is only logical, for the Lord revealed that all would perish but Noah and his family; however, Enoch knew it, and was honored by it, before any of the destruction. [99]

The Lord Revealed to Enoch that Jesus
Christ Would Be Crucified

From Adam to Enoch, many knew that the Redeemer would live and die. Yet, there is no evidence that anyone before Enoch knew specifically how the Savior would die. Enoch received two visions on the subject. He saw Jesus Christ's day and testified, "the Righteous is lifted up, and the Lamb is slain" (Moses 7:47). Enoch described the Redeemer's death in his second vision even more specifically, "And the Lord said unto Enoch: Look, and he looked and beheld the Son of Man lifted up on the cross, after the manner of men" (Moses 7:55). Enoch clearly saw how Jesus Christ's life would end. Significantly, the Bible includes prophecies of the Crucifixion, but none are as deep and expansive as Enoch's vision, and they all were written after Enoch's time. [100] The only prophecy that matches Enoch's vivid vision is in the Book of Mormon. Thousands of years after Enoch, Nephi also saw the Savior lifted up on the cross (see 1 Nephi 11:33).[101] The Lord inspired Joseph Smith to add the first biblical reference to Jesus Christ's Crucifixion. In fact, it is also the only specific, vivid, Old Testament vision of the Savior on the cross. [102]

It is noteworthy that in the same month that Joseph Smith added the vision of Enoch to the Bible, he recorded the Lord's words in revelation that testified, "I am Jesus Christ, the Son of God, who was crucified for the sins of the world, even as many as will believe on my name, that they may become the sons of God" (D&C 35:2). The Doctrine and Covenants already included the Lord's testimony of His Crucifixion (see D&C 6:37; 20:23; 21:9). Over the next year and two months, the Lord would testify of this event another five times (see D&C 45:52; 46:13; 53:2; 54:1; 76:41). These revelations taught that it is a gift of the Spirit "to know that Jesus Christ is the Son of God, and that he was crucified for the sins of the world" (D&C 46:13). Enoch certainly had this gift.

The Earth Testifies of
the Atonement

As Enoch learned about the Atonement, he discovered that the earth itself is alive. It cried out in his vision because of the pain and wickedness of men. It asked, "When will my Creator sanctify me" (Moses 7:48). The Bible testifies that the Fall was not exclusive to mankind.

The earth also felt its effects. The ground was cursed; it would bring forth thorns and thistles, and man would have to work to gain food (see Genesis 3:17–18; Moses 4:23–24). The JST adds that not only did the earth feel these effects, but it also felt the wickedness and filthiness of its inhabitants. Enoch, hearing this, asked the Father in the name of the Son to have mercy on the earth and Noah's posterity.

Enoch asked if the earth would rest when Jesus Christ first came (see Moses 7:54). According to the JST, Enoch then witnessed a vision of the Crucifixion. Truly it was a time of "wickedness and vengeance" as the Lord had already told Enoch, and the earth would not rest (Moses 7:46). In fact, Enoch saw that "all the creations of God mourned; and the earth groaned; and the rocks were rent" (Moses 7:56). The earth would physically react to its Creator's death. Enoch saw the destruction that is recorded in the Book of Mormon thousands of years before it happened (see 3 Nephi 8).

Interestingly, the Doctrine and Covenants revisited many of the same images of Enoch's vision in September of 1832. It revealed that in latter-day times, "the whole world lieth in sin, and groaneth under darkness and under the bondage of sin . . . the whole world groaneth under sin and darkness even now" (D&C 84:49, 53). This could be interpreted as saying that both the earth itself and its inhabitants feel this darkness and bondage.

Enoch learned that the earth would finally rest for 1,000 years when Jesus Christ returned at His Second Coming (see Moses 7:64). The Doctrine and Covenants revealed much more on this subject as time passed. In March of 1832, Joseph Smith recorded that in the beginning of this millennial period "will the Lord God sanctify the earth . . . and judge all things, and shall redeem all things, except that which he hath not put into his power" (D&C 77:12). By virtue of the fact that the earth will be sanctified, it is safe to say that it is in "his power," or under the power of the Atonement. On December 27, 1832, Joseph Smith recorded why. The revelation he received taught that the earth would be redeemed and glorified because it "filleth the measure of its creation, and transgresseth not the law" (D&C 88:25). It was and is obedient to God. "Wherefore, it shall be sanctified . . . and the righteous shall inherit it" (D&C 88:26).

The earth projects a pattern for how man can use the Atonement of Jesus Christ. God created the earth. The Flood symbolized a baptism.

It was obedient to God. In the Doctrine and Covenants, the Lord even specifically stated, "it shall die" (D&C 88:26). The same revelation continues, "it shall be quickened again, and shall abide the power by which it is quickened" (D&C 88:26).[103] In other words, the earth will pass away and then gain celestial glory (see D&C 88:25–29). Joseph Smith taught, "We believe . . . that the earth will be renewed and receive its paradisiacal glory" (Article of Faith 10), and "This earth will be rolled back into the presence of God, and crowned with celestial glory"[104]

An immense power has to be in action for such a change in the earth itself. Joseph Smith recorded on February 16, 1832, that the Lord "came into the world, even Jesus, to be crucified for the world, and to bear the sins of the world, and to sanctify the world, and to cleanse it from all unrighteousness" (D&C 76:41). The most immediate application of this verse refers to mankind; however, it also refers to the world, or earth itself. Joseph Smith wrote in his poetic commentary of this revelation, "he came to the world . . . to lay down his life . . . and sanctify earth for a blessed repose. 'Tis decreed, that he'll [Jesus Christ] save all the work of his hands, and sanctify them by his own precious blood."[105] The Atonement did not only pay for the sins of man, but also for the fallen earth itself.

The Lord Revealed to Enoch the Effects of the Atonement on Those Who Have Died

Still speaking of the effects of the Atonement on the earth, Enoch saw that at the time of Jesus Christ's death and Resurrection that "as many of the spirits as were in prison came forth, and stood on the right hand of God; and the remainder were reserved in chains of darkness until the judgment of the great day" (Moses 7:57). There were clearly two different groups which would be polarized during this event. Some spirits "came forth." They left prison, or in other words, they were resurrected. Other spirits remained in prison and in darkness until judgment. According to the JST, Enoch knew there would be an order to the resurrection. The righteous would resurrect first, beginning with Jesus Christ. Others would have to stay in prison until judgment. Enoch also saw that "the saints arose, and were crowned at the right hand of the Son of Man, with crowns of glory" (Moses 7:56). The righteous that were resurrected at the time of Christ would be crowned and receive their reward of glory.

Joseph Smith recorded that the Lord testified, "and righteousness will I send down out of heaven; and truth will I send forth out of the earth, to bear testimony of mine Only Begotten; his resurrection from the dead; yea, and also the resurrection of all men" (Moses 7:62).[106] The Lord promised to use divinely prepared ways to testify of His Resurrection. At the very time the Lord revealed this prophecy through Joseph Smith, it was partially fulfilled. The Lord promised to send righteousness out of heaven to testify of the resurrection. If "righteousness" refers to people that would come out of heaven, Joseph Smith received many great testimonies. Jesus Christ Himself appeared with the Father to Joseph Smith. There is no greater testimony of the Resurrection. Moroni, John the Baptist, Peter, and James all appeared to Joseph Smith in their resurrected forms. If "righteousness" is interpreted as revelation, Joseph Smith received many great examples (as this book demonstrates).

According to the JST, the Lord also promised that "truth will I send forth out of the earth" to bear record of Jesus Christ and the Resurrection. Moroni guided Joseph Smith to gold plates, which were buried in the ground. Fittingly, this book testifies over and over of Jesus Christ and His Resurrection. There are over fifty Book of Mormon references that specifically and directly testify of the reality of Jesus Christ's power over death and of His Resurrection. The climax of the account comes with the appearance of the resurrected Savior to those in the Americas. [107]

REVELATIONS ABOUT THE ATONEMENT
DECEMBER 1830

1. Enoch preached a very instructive sermon on the Fall and its effects.

2. Adam utilized the Atonement through baptism.

3. Children are redeemed from the Fall by the Atonement.

4. Enoch used symbols of water, spirit, and blood to teach about the Atonement.

5. The Atonement empowered Jesus Christ to be mankind's advocate.

6. The Lord revealed to Enoch that the Savior would come after the Flood, and he saw Jesus Christ's coming and Atonement.

7. The Lord revealed to Enoch that the Savior would come through his lineage.

8. The Lord revealed to Enoch that Jesus Christ would be crucified.

9. The earth testified of the Atonement.

10. The Lord revealed to Enoch the effects of the Atonement on the dead.

Chapter 4

REVELATIONS ABOUT THE
ATONEMENT IN 1831

———————————— ❧ ————————————

IN JANUARY OF 1831, THE CHURCH had only been organized for nine months, and yet the Prophet Joseph Smith received another thirty-seven revelations that would come to be included in the Doctrine and Covenants (see D&C 1; 38–72; 133). He felt to make many pivotal changes regarding what the Old Testament records the prophets knew about the Atonement. The Prophet then received inspiration to postpone his work with the Old Testament in order to work on the New Testament. The Lord inspired Joseph Smith to make additions and corrections to the entire book of Matthew in 1831. Jesus Christ's life and mission were central to Matthew's Gospel and the corresponding inspired changes.

January–February 1831

At the end of 1830, a revelation commanded the Church to move to Ohio, and instructed Joseph Smith to stop his work with the Bible until he arrived there (see D&C 37:1). "About the first of February," Joseph and Emma finished their 300-mile journey in harsh winter. [108] On February 4, 1831, the Lord directed the Saints to build a house for the Prophet to live in and continue his Bible translation, which would then resume (see D&C 41:7). Between February 1, and March 8, 1831, the Lord guided Joseph Smith in making corrections and additions from about Genesis 5:29 to Genesis 19:35.[109] As the majority of these changes probably took place in February, they will be discussed with that month. These changes showed what the Old Testament prophets knew about the Atonement. Also in January and February, the Prophet Joseph received seven revelations that are currently found in the Doctrine and Covenants. January was mainly a month of travel and transition. February brought much understanding on the resurrection, Old Testament views on the Atonement, and the Atonement's unconditional mercy for children.

The Resurrection of the Just and the Resurrection of the Unjust

One revelation received in February of 1831 taught that the Lord still has power over death today. It declared that in the Lord's timing sometimes the righteous die, but, in His words, "those that die in me shall not taste of death, for it shall be sweet unto them" (D&C 42:46). It also taught that death is different for the wicked, "And they that die not in me, wo unto them, for their death is bitter" (D&C 42:47). The revelation instructed the Saints to weep for those that die, but "more especially for those that have not hope of a glorious resurrection" (D&C 42:45). Thus, even though they may die in like manner, there is a vivid difference between what is experienced in the death of the righteous versus that of the wicked.

There must be different kinds of resurrections, if there is a "glorious resurrection" that not all will receive. Concepts of a first or just resurrection, and a later or unjust resurrection are taught in the Bible (see Luke 14:14; John 5:29; Acts 24:15; Revelation 20:5–6).[110] However, the biblical verses offer no explanation of who will qualify for the first or just resurrection. Joseph Smith had previously translated these words from the Book of Mormon prophet Abinadi that clarified the subject:

> And there cometh a resurrection, even a first resurrection; yea, even a resurrection of those that have been, and who are, and who shall be, even until the resurrection of Christ—for so shall he be called.
>
> And now, the resurrection of all the prophets, and all those that have believed in their words, or all those that have kept the

commandments of God, shall come forth in the first resurrection; therefore, they are the first resurrection.

They are raised to dwell with God who has redeemed them; thus they have eternal life through Christ who has broken the bands of death.

And these are those who have part in the first resurrection; and these are they that have died before Christ came, in their ignorance, not having salvation declared unto them. And thus the Lord bringeth about the restoration of these; and they have a part in the first resurrection, or have eternal life, being redeemed by the Lord. (Mosiah 15:21–24) [111]

Abinadi defined "the just" in the first resurrection as the prophets, and those who followed them and kept the commandments. Interestingly, the just will also include those who died before Jesus lived who did not hear the gospel. In March of 1831, a revelation repeated the teaching about the latter group: "they that knew no law shall have part in the first resurrection; and it shall be tolerable for them" (D&C 45:54). The doctrine that those who were ignorant of the gospel in life will take part in the first resurrection teaches us something important about the Lord and the Atonement. The Lord will reward those who lived His laws and used His Atonement, and will punish those who knew His laws but did not live them. The fact that the ignorant will rise with the righteous shows the breadth of the Lord's mercy. They will not be punished for what they did not know.

Over a year later, in December of 1832, the Lord revealed even more through Joseph Smith on the first resurrection. This revelation taught that the first resurrection would be divided into two parts. It will be in the second portion of the first resurrection that those who were ignorant of the gospel will rise. The revelation referred to them as those "who have received their part in that prison which is prepared for them, that they might receive the gospel" (D&C 88:99). Those who did not have the gospel must learn it, in their spirit state, in prison. They cannot skip those steps. After accepting the gospel, they will be allowed to resurrect with the just.

In August of 1831, further revelation listed traits of those who would not be included in this first or glorious resurrection, those who were defined as the fearful, the unbelieving, liars, and whoremongers

(see D&C 63:17–18). The Lord reiterated that there would be two resurrections, then stated that "for this cause preached the apostles unto
the world the resurrection of the dead" (D&C 63:52). The Lord wants
as many as possible to participate in the glorious first resurrection.

Noah Preached the Gospel
of Jesus Christ

During February of 1831, the Lord inspired Joseph Smith to make
some pivotal corrections and additions to the story of Noah. According
to the Bible, Noah "found grace in the eyes of the Lord" so he and his
family were saved from the Flood (Genesis 6:8). The biblical account
recorded Noah preparing the ark and the animals, but there is no mention of any attempt to save anyone other than Noah's family. It is as if
the Flood was a great secret. The JST made substantial changes to this
account. In the JST, the Lord called Noah to "declare his Gospel unto
the children of men" (Moses 8:19). Noah tried: "And it came to pass
that Noah called upon the children of men that they should repent;
but they hearkened not unto his words" (Moses 8:20). One string of
rejections did not stop Noah. He persisted in his missionary efforts.
"Noah continued his preaching . . . saying . . . Believe and repent of
your sins and be baptized in the name of Jesus Christ, the Son of God,
even as our fathers, and ye shall receive the Holy Ghost, that ye may
have all things made manifest; and if ye do not this, the floods will
come in upon you; nevertheless they hearkened not" (Moses 8:23–24).
In the JST, it is clear that Noah understood the gospel just as Adam
and Enoch did, and that he shared it as they did. He knew about the
Atonement that would happen, and encouraged his people to repent
and be baptized to utilize its power. Unfortunately, their rejection of
the gospel, of the Atonement, and of Noah's message, led to the monumental tragedy of the Flood. [112]

The Lord Revealed Details through Joseph Smith about
Melchizedek That Pertain to the Atonement

In February of 1831, the Lord also inspired Joseph Smith to add a fascinating insight to the account of two other Old Testament prophets,
Melchizedek and Abraham. There are few biblical details about
Melchizedek. In fact, in the Bible, he appears to be a mystical king
and priest who was never born, nor will ever die, who met and blessed

Abraham, who accepted tithing from Abraham, who Jesus Christ Himself was a high priest after his order (see Genesis 14:18–20; Hebrews 5:6; 7:1–3).[113] In the KJV, after Abraham courageously rescued his nephew Lot, Melchizedek met with Abraham and brought bread and water. The JST added that Melchizedek "break bread and blest it; and he blest the wine" (JST Genesis 14:18). The JST then makes the connection that Melchizedek needed to be "the priest of the most high God" to do such an act (JST Genesis 14:18). To the modern reader, this is a curious occurrence. The sacrament is usually viewed as an inspired outgrowth of the Passover. However, it appears as though this inspired Old Testament passage taught that the sacrament was observed among those with the proper priesthood authority hundreds of years before the Passover, and thousands of years before the Savior's mortality.[114]

There is support for this idea to be found in Joseph Smith's teachings. As has been previously noted, Joseph Smith taught that from the beginning there were more ordinances than just blood sacrifice: "We all admit that the Gospel has ordinances, and if so, had it not always ordinances, and were not its ordinances always the same?"[115] Joseph Smith explained that the gospel and its ordinances were known long before Jesus Christ's day. The ancients were not ignorant of them. It appears as though those in certain positions in the Old Testament were not ignorant of the sacrament. There is no indication of such a practice in the Old Testament without the JST.

The Lord also revealed in the JST that sometime after this meeting between Melchizedek and Abraham, that Melchizedek's people "wrought righteousness, and obtained heaven" just like the city of Enoch (JST Genesis 14:24). Melchizedek had to perform great miracles in order for this to happen. But he and his people were yet another success story. Mankind can use the Atonement and follow "the will of the Son of God which was from before the foundation of the world" until they are safely saved (JST Genesis 14:24).

Abraham had a Testimony of the Resurrection

The JST adds further insight to Abraham's story as well. In the Bible, the Lord made some dramatic promises to the ancient patriarch. He promised that Abraham's seed would be innumerable like the stars of the sky, and that he would inherit certain land. The JST added, "And Abram said, Lord God, how wilt thou give me this land for an everlasting inheritance? And the Lord said, Though thou wast dead, yet am I not able to give it thee? And if thou shalt die, yet thou shalt possess it, for the day cometh, that the Son of Man shall live; but how can he live if he be not dead? he must first be quickened" (JST Genesis 15:5). The Lord expanded Abraham's vision to help him realize that death would not stop divine promises. As the Savior would resurrect, so would Abraham. So would his descendants. The Abrahamic covenant could only be an "everlasting inheritance" through the Resurrection of Jesus Christ. Surely Abraham had a testimony of the Resurrection.

The JST also adds, "and it came to pass, that Abram looked forth and saw the days of the Son of Man [Jesus Christ], and was glad, and his soul found rest" (JST Genesis 15:6). Again, another Old Testament prophet saw the days of the Savior. Again, the testimony had a great effect on him. Interestingly, there is no direct mention of the Redeemer in all the KJV story of Abraham.

People of Abraham's Time Distorted Doctrine and Ordinances Regarding the Atonement

The JST also adds more insight to the people of Abraham's time. God told Abraham, "My people have gone astray from my precepts, and have not kept mine ordinances, which I gave unto their fathers; and they have not observed mine anointing, and the burial, or baptism wherewith I commanded them; but have turned from the commandment, and taken unto themselves the washing of children, and the blood of sprinkling" (JST Genesis 17:3). They had distorted the practice of baptism, which was supposed to symbolize a burial. Paul taught that immersion in water symbolized Jesus Christ's burial and coming out of the water symbolized the Resurrection. He also taught that immersion symbolized the Atonement's application to the person being baptized. The burial symbolized the death or burial of a person's sins, and returning from the water symbolized the same person's newness of life (see Romans 6:4–8). The people of Abraham's time wrongly resorted to a baptism of sprinkling, which changed the symbolism of the Atonement.[116]

It is important to note that according to the JST, God revealed that these people had erroneously "taken unto themselves the washing of children" (JST Genesis 17:3). Chronologically, this is the first mention in recorded scripture where little children were incorrectly baptized. Previous to 1831, Joseph Smith had translated in the Book of Mormon that baptizing little children is a "solemn mockery" before the Lord, "denying the mercies of Christ" (Moroni 8:9, 23). He also translated King Benjamin's sermon that taught that the Atonement covered the sins of these little ones (see Mosiah 3:16). Joseph Smith had also previously recorded in April of 1830 that only those who had "arrived unto the years of accountability before God" and were "capable of repentance" could enter Church membership (D&C 20:71).

In contrast to these teachings revealed through Joseph Smith, many other influential religious voices taught infant baptism. George Whitefield taught "putting the infants under the water signified their obligation to die unto sin; as their taking them out of the water, signified their rising again to newness of life." [117] John Welsey taught, "It is certain our Church supposes that all who are baptized in their infancy are at the same time born again; and it is allowed that the whole Office for the Baptism of Infants proceeds upon this supposition. . . . We cannot comprehend how this work can be wrought in infants." [118]

In the JST, God also taught that the people of Abraham's time "have said that the blood of the righteous Abel was shed for sins; and have not known wherein they are accountable before me" (JST Genesis 17:3). They had distorted the doctrine of the Atonement. Instead of looking forward to a Savior, they attributed the great saving act to Abel, a mere mortal, who had been murdered. In essence, the people of Abraham's day removed Jesus Christ from their worship, and the Lord commanded them to repent.

Children Are Saved in the Atonement until Eight Years Old

Later in this story of Abraham, the JST added to the Bible the first revelation indicating exactly when children should be held accountable and baptized. The Lord told Abraham, "thou mayest know for ever that children are not accountable before me until they are eight years old" (JST Genesis 17:7). Clearly this testimony condemned the incorrect practice of infant baptism. It also gave insight to the practice of circumcision. The Lord had Abraham, and those that followed, circumcise their sons at eight days old as a symbol of the covenant those same sons would make at eight years old. Of course, this addition also indicated that Abraham, like the prophets before him, correctly practiced the ordinance of baptism.

About nine months later, in November 1831, Joseph Smith recorded a revelation that reminded the Church that children were not held accountable and should not be baptized until eight years old (see D&C 68:27). This same revelation taught that if parents did not teach their children "the doctrine of repentance, faith in Christ the Son of the living God, and of baptism and the gift of the Holy Ghost by the laying on of the hands, when eight years old, the sin be upon the heads of the parents" (D&C 68:25). Children leave the completely protective care of the Atonement when they turn eight. After that, they are accountable for sin. According to the revelation, parents must teach them how to enter back into that care through faith in the Savior, repentance, baptism, and receiving the Holy Ghost. A careful reading of Doctrine and Covenants 68:24–27 suggests that God had already revealed this doctrine. He had indeed, through the JST.

Those Living at the Second Coming Will Be Resurrected at Their Appointed Time

The Apostle Paul taught that some would not die, but would be changed "in the twinkling of an eye" (1 Corinthians 15:52). In February of 1831, Joseph Smith recorded a repetition of this teaching, delineating that it would happen only to the righteous during the Millennium (see D&C 43:32).[119] Six months later, revelation continued on the subject by teaching that such righteous people have a determined time to live before their resurrection. They will die at the "age of man," children will live to be "old," and the old "shall not sleep in the dust, but they shall be changed in the twinkling of an eye" (D&C 63:50–51). This was the Lord's commentary on Isaiah 65:20–22.

REVELATIONS ABOUT THE ATONEMENT JANUARY–FEBRUARY 1831

1. There will be a resurrection of the just and a resurrection of the unjust, and those who died without the

law and the gospel will resurrect with the just, if they accept the gospel in the hereafter.

2. Long before the Flood, Noah relentlessly urged his people to utilize the Atonement by repenting.

3. Old Testament prophets observed the sacrament.

4. Through the Atonement, Melchizedek and his people were translated.

5. The Lord taught Abraham about the Resurrection, and Abraham saw Jesus Christ's ministry.

6. People in Abraham's time wrongly distorted doctrines and practices regarding the Atonement by baptizing by sprinkling, baptizing children, and claiming Abel's blood was shed for a remission of sins.

7. Children are saved and covered by the Atonement until eight years old.

8. Those living at the Second Coming will be resurrected at their appointed time.

arch 1831

During March of 1831, Joseph Smith recorded five revelations that are now included in the Doctrine and Covenants (see D&C 45–49). In one of these revelations, the Lord directed Joseph Smith to leave his work in the Old Testament and begin in the New Testament (see D&C 45:60–61). The Prophet obediently began his new assignment in the first chapter of Matthew. By April 7, he had worked through to Matthew 9:2.[120] Revelation in March taught that all prophets testified of Jesus Christ, strengthened the testimonies of New Testament figures on Jesus Christ, prophesied of the Jews' realization that Jesus is the Christ, clarified what the young mortal Savior knew about His sacrifice, and taught on the order of the resurrection.

Existence between Death and
Resurrection Is a Bondage

Revelations received in March of 1831 set the foundation for insights on another important aspect of the Atonement. The Lord revealed teachings he gave His Apostles in Jerusalem during His mortality. In one conversation not recorded in the New Testament, the Apostles thought the time between their deaths and the Second Coming "to be a bondage" (D&C 45:17). In many ways they had reason for their feelings. Over two years later Joseph Smith recorded more on the subject: "For man is spirit. The elements are eternal, and spirit and element, inseparably connected, receive a fullness of joy; and when separated, man cannot receive a fullness of joy" (D&C 93:33–34). The Atonement allows us to leave the bondage of the spirit world, resurrect, and receive this fullness of joy.

The Righteous Will Resurrect before the Destruction of the Wicked

Still in March of 1831, revelation described the first resurrection. It began with the Resurrection of Jesus Christ and continued through His Second Coming. The Lord revealed through Joseph Smith that "before the arm of the Lord shall fall, an angel shall sound his trump, and the saints that have slept shall come forth ["from the four quarters of the earth" (D&C 45:46)] to meet me [the Lord] in the cloud" (D&C 45:45). This revelation taught that the first resurrection at the time of His Second Coming would begin before the destruction of the wicked.[121] The righteous will be lifted to meet the Savior. Many Christians call this the "Rapture."

Just a month or two later the Lord inspired Joseph Smith to add this concept to the New Testament parable of the wheat and the tares. The parable in the KJV stated that God will let both the wheat [the righteous] and the tares [the wicked] grow together, but instructed, "gather together first the tares" or the wicked (Matthew 13:30). The order is reversed in the JST. God instructs, "gather ye together first the wheat into my barn; and the tares are bound in bundles to be burned" (JST Matthew 13:30). There is another place where this order can be interpreted from the Bible, 1 Thessalonians 4:15–17.[122] The JST and the Doctrine and Covenants taught how the Atonement would raise the righteous from their graves before the destruction of the world, or before the Millennium.

A Prophecy that the Jews Will Accept
Jesus Christ as Their Savior

Also in March of 1831, Joseph Smith recorded clarification of an Old Testament prophecy. Zechariah spoke of a day when "one shall say unto him, What are these wounds in thine hands? Then he shall answer, Those with which I was wounded in the house of my friends" (Zechariah 13:6). Zecharaiah also prophesied that Jesus Christ would come in glory and miraculously save the Jews (see Zecharaiah 14:1–5). In March, Joseph Smith recorded words the Lord spoke in his Olivet discourse to His Apostles in New Testament times on this subject. This portion of the sermon is not found in the Bible. In this revelation, the Lord instructs that He will save the Jews:

> *Then shall the Jews look upon me and say: What are these wounds in thine hands and in thy feet? Then shall they know that I am the Lord; for I will say unto them: These wounds are the wounds with which I was wounded in the house of my friends. I am he who was lifted up. I am Jesus that was crucified. I am the Son of God. And then shall they weep because of their iniquities; then shall they lament because they persecuted their king.* (D&C 45:51–53)

It is important to note that in this prophecy it does not mention that the Jews would understand that their Savior was and is Jesus of Nazareth. They would be curious about the marks of the nails in His hands and feet, the symbols of His famous death. This is not to say they would be naïve to what happened, but this would be a moment of awakening concerning His sacrifice. According to the revelation, this prophecy will be fulfilled when the Savior returns to Jerusalem as part of His Second Coming.

It may be important to also discuss the Jews generally. According to recently discussed revelation, which is now Doctrine and Covenants forty-five, the Jews would feel grief "because of their iniquities." One way to understand this phrase would involve their personal sorrow for all of their personal sin. Also, they will "lament because they persecuted their king." Their ancestors were the key figures in the Savior's death. This does not state that later generations of Jews are responsible for the Crucifixion, but that they would lament. Their ancestors passed down beliefs and traditions that Jesus was not the Christ. This could likely be part of the persecution of the Savior they will lament.[123] It is important to note that the revelation did not say that each Jew was responsible for Jesus Christ's death. Their ancestors were also Apostles and stalwart Church members. Jesus Christ Himself was a Jew.

Several months later on November 3, 1831, Joseph Smith recorded, "and they also of the tribe of Judah, after their pain, shall be sanctified in holiness before the Lord, to dwell in his presence day and night, forever and ever" (D&C 133:35). The Jews will feel for their iniquities and for Jesus Christ's death, but the Atonement covers and will save the Jews that will come to the Savior and accept Him as the Messiah.

Multiple Prophets Testified of Jesus Christ's Birth

Immediately after Joseph Smith received Doctrine and Covenants forty-five in March of 1831, he began his work on the book of Matthew. Matthew began his Gospel with a genealogical account and then a quick summary of the Savior's birth.[124] He then testified that Jesus Christ would "save his people from their sins" (Matthew 1:21). He continued, "Now all this was done that it might be fulfilled which was spoken of the Lord by the prophet, saying . . ." and Matthew quotes scripture which closely resembles Isaiah 7:14 (Matthew 1:22). The JST made a small but significant alteration. It changed the word prophet to "prophets" (JST Matthew 1:22). If the Son of God, the future Savior of the world, would be miraculously born of a virgin, it stands to reason that the Lord would reveal it to more than one prophet. With the JST change, Matthew appears to have written that many prophets prophesied similarly to Isaiah. There are no other verses in the KJV Old Testament that speak of a virgin giving birth. Interestingly, there are no other verses in the JST either. There are, however, such prophecies in the Book of Mormon (see 1 Nephi 11:13–20; Alma 7:10). There is also a record of Nephi quoting Isaiah 7:14 exactly (see 2 Nephi 17:14). With that statement alone, there were two prophets that prophesied using the same words of the Savior's birth. Perhaps Nephi was not the only other prophet to do so. Matthew likely did not have access to the Book of Mormon record. Surely other prophets knew and prophesied, or repeated Isaiah's prophecy that Jesus Christ, the Son of God, would be born of a virgin.

Herod Knew of the Prophets'
Testimonies of Jesus Christ

The JST attributed knowledge of such prophecies to Herod the Great, the same man who tried to kill the infant Savior. When the wise men came to Bethlehem searching for the infant Jesus, Herod called his chief priests and scribes demanding "of them where Christ should be born" (Matthew 2:4). The JST added an insightful change to Herod's question, "Where *is the place that is written of by the prophets, in which* Christ should be born?" (JST Matthew 2:4; italics indicate changes from the KJV text). According to the JST, Herod knew of the prophecies of the Savior before the wise men came, though it would seem he did not believe them (see JST Matthew 2:4). The priests responded to Herod's demand, not explaining prophecies of "a Governor" who would "rule" during his mortal ministry as the KJV states, but "the Messiah" who would "save" (Matthew 2:4; JST Matthew 2:4).

Included in the JST account of Herod and his wise men is another interesting commentary on previous prophets. Three times in this account the JST revealed that "prophets," not just a prophet, prophesied that the Son of God would be born in Bethlehem (see JST Matthew 2:4–5). Also in the JST, the chief priests and scribes quoted the prophets as saying, "The word of the Lord came unto *us*, saying . . ." (JST Matthew 2:4, emphasis added). This was another plural reference to prophets. The JST indicates that more than one prophet gave this prophecy.

The prophecy that Herod's wise men quoted to him is very similar to Micah 5:2, which is the only Old Testament verse that specifically prophesied that the Redeemer would be born in Bethlehem. However, with the JST changes, there are many similarities and many differences between the quotation in Matthew and in Micah:

> But thou, Beth-lehem Ephratah, though thou be little among the thousands of Judah, yet out of thee shall he come forth unto me that is to be ruler in Israel; whose goings forth have been from of old, from everlasting. (Micah 5:2)

> And thou Bethlehem, which lieth in the land of Judea, in thee shall be born a prince, which art not the least among the princes of Judea: for out of thee shall come the Messiah, who shall save my people Israel. (JST Matthew 2:6)

The greatest difference occurs at the end of the verse where, in the JST, the prophecy of the Atonement is clear. Interestingly the Micah account is left untouched in the JST, but this correction in Matthew could be considered divine clarification to Micah 5:2.[125]

Jesus Christ Knew Many Years Before His Ministry of His Atonement

The young Jesus Christ would have read the words of Old Testament prophets who testified of a Redeemer to come. It is possible to ask if Jesus Christ needed to learn that He would be the Savior. If so, when did He realize it? Luke wrote that, "Jesus increased in wisdom" (Luke 2:52). In order to increase in wisdom, one cannot already know everything. This question cannot be answered perfectly, however Joseph Smith recorded many insights on the issue.

In March of 1831, the JST added to Matthew that "many years" before the Savior's ministry, He "needed not that any man should teach him" and "neither could he be taught" (JST Matthew 2:23). In a time of famous minds such as Gamaliel, Jesus Christ "increased in wisdom" beyond them. If "many years" before the Savior began his ministry, He had progressed intellectually beyond any other person, He must have known that He would atone for all mankind. Many others such as Mary, Joseph, the shepherds, Simeon, Anna, and the Wise Men, also knew that He would save the world.

From late 1831 to early 1832, Joseph Smith felt inspired to make corrections to Luke's account of twelve-year-old Jesus in the temple speaking with the doctors. According to the Prophet, the young Savior was not "hearing them, and asking them questions" as the KJV recorded, but "they were hearing *him*, and asking *him* questions" (Luke 2:46; JST Luke 2:46, emphasis added). Perhaps at age twelve no man could teach Jesus Christ. [126] Whether at age 12 or older, according to the JST, "many years" before Jesus Christ's ministry, He knew He would atone for the world.

John the Baptist Testified of the Savior More Boldly than is Recorded in the KJV

Much has been written about John the Baptist as being a forerunner, the one who would prepare the way for the atoning Savior. The most obvious way that he prepared for Jesus Christ was by baptizing, and he baptized "many" in Judea (JST Matthew 3:6; see Mark 1:5). John's father, Zacharias, prophesied when his son was eight days old that he would "give knowledge of salvation unto his people for the remission of their sins" (Luke 1:77). The JST added that Zacharias prophesied that John would accomplish this "by baptism" (JST Luke 1:77).[127]

In the New Testament, John grew to be a powerful figure, boldly testifying of Jesus Christ. During March of 1831, the JST heightened and clarified John's testimony in several instances. John described Jesus Christ as "he of whom I bear record," and "he of whom I shall bear record" (JST Matthew 3:11–12). John the Baptist frankly testified to the Pharisees and Sadducees, "If ye receive not me, ye receive not him of whom I am sent to bear record" (JST Matthew 3:8). One of the most famous passages in which John bears testimony of the Savior is recorded in the KJV. He stated, "[Jesus Christ] is mightier than I, whose shoes I am not worthy to bear" (Matthew 3:11). The JST added John's explanation of this phrase, "or whose place I am not able to fill" (JST Matthew 3:11; JST John 1:27). As great as John the Baptist was, he understood and testified that he could not take Jesus Christ's place as Savior.

As time went on, the JST added that the Savior testified of the connection between John's teachings and Himself: "For he that believed not John concerning me, cannot believe me, except he first repent. And except ye repent, the preaching of John shall condemn you in the day of judgment" (JST Matthew 21:32).[128] The JST elevated John's role and testimony in content and importance. Jesus taught of John's testimony, "And he [John] received not his testimony of man, but of God . . . therefore ye ought to receive his testimony" (JST John 5:34). Interestingly, the JST also indicated that "many received John as a prophet, but they believed not on Jesus" (JST John 4:1). This detail shows selective belief by some of John's followers, for John clearly testified of the Savior.

A spiritual highlight in John's life was his experience of baptizing the Savior. In March of 1831, the JST added a few words that personalized the experience for John. After the baptism, the JST stated, "*and John saw*, and lo, the heavens were opened unto him, and he saw the Spirit of God descending like a dove, and lighting upon *Jesus*: And lo, *he* [John] *heard* a voice from heaven, saying, This is my beloved Son, in whom I am well pleased. *Hear ye him*" (JST Matthew 3:15, italics indicate JST changes; compare Matthew 3:16–17). Whether others saw the Holy Ghost or heard the voice, the account does not specify, but John saw and heard. He knew that Jesus Christ was the Son of God. The Father instructed John to listen to the Savior. Surely some unmentioned teaching followed. John's reluctance to baptize the Savior indicated that he knew who Jesus Christ was before the baptism; however, John knew it by divine manifestation after the ordinance.

The Lord, through the JST, later clarified an important passage regarding John. Twice in the beginning chapter of John, while the Baptist related the story of baptizing the Savior, he stated, "And I knew him not" (John 1:31, 33). The JST removed the word "not" in both passages (JST John 1:31, 33). The first alteration indicated that John knew the Savior before the day of baptism. The second not only indicated that John was familiar with Jesus, but suggests that perhaps Jesus had taught him of the sign of the dove previous to the baptism (see JST John 1:32–33).[129]

All Prophets Testified
of Jesus Christ

As has been previously discussed, the Lord revealed through Joseph Smith that Old Testament prophets clearly knew that a Savior would come and atone the sins of all mankind. From Adam on, they all prophesied of Jesus Christ. Those who lived in the Redeemer's day had many of the prophets' writings. In fact, the JST adds a powerful phrase in the fourth chapter of Matthew when Jesus Christ called Peter and Andrew to follow Him, "*I am he of whom it is written by the prophets;* follow me, and I will make you fishers of men" (JST Matthew 4:19; italics indicate JST changes). The Savior used scripture to testify of his status as the Messiah. He also chose men who were likely familiar with Old Testament writings, and who were looking for a Savior. They believed that He was the Messiah written of anciently (see Matthew 4:20).

Joseph Smith had already recorded a bold teaching on this subject in the Book of Mormon. Abinadi taught: all the prophets who have prophesied ever since the world began [have testified] . . . that God himself should come down among the children of men . . . [and] he should bring to pass the resurrection of the dead, and that he, himself, should be oppressed and afflicted (Mosiah 13:33–35). Whether or not each scriptural account demonstrated a particular prophet's testimony of Jesus Christ, each prophet had one and shared it.

The JST adds many further references to the New Testament that validate the fact that ancient prophets testified of the Savior. In the JST, John the Baptist's disciples asked Jesus Christ, "Art thou he of whom it is written in the prophets that he should come" (JST Matthew 11:3). The JST adds that the Savior chastised the Pharisees with these words, "Ye know not Moses, neither the prophets; for if ye had known them, ye would have believed on me; for to this intent they were written. For I am sent that ye might have life" (JST Luke 14:34). Two verses later, the JST explains, "These things he said, signifying that which was written, verily must all be fulfilled" (JST Luke 14:35). At least eight other references changed in the JST of the New Testament reestablished that the Savior came in fulfillment of earlier prophecies (see JST Matthew 2:4; 4:19; 11:13–14; 23:39; JST Luke 3:5–7; 16:16–18; 22:16; JST John 3:18).[130] A few of these examples will be discussed later individually.

REVELATIONS ABOUT THE ATONEMENT
MARCH 1831

1. Existence between death and resurrection is a type of bondage.

2. The righteous will resurrect before the destruction of the wicked.

3. The Jews will grieve because of their iniquities and finally accept Jesus Christ as their Savior.

4. Multiple prophets, not just Isaiah, prophesied of Jesus Christ's miraculous birth.

5. Herod and his wise men declared that multiple prophets, in addition to Micah, prophesied that Jesus Christ would be born in Bethlehem.

6. Jesus Christ knew many years before his ministry began that He would complete the Atonement for all mankind.

7. John the Baptist testified of the Savior more boldly than is recorded in the KJV.

8. All true prophets testified of Jesus Christ.

April–July 1831

From April to July of 1831, Joseph Smith received eight revelations that are recorded in the Doctrine and Covenants (see D&C 50–57). He had also been simultaneously working on his biblical translation; he wrote, "During the month of April, I continued to translate the Scriptures as time would allow." [131] Of the few recorded dates dealing with the JST, it is evident that from April 7 to July 19, Joseph Smith made corrections and additions from Matthew 9:2 to Matthew 26:71.[132] The Lord continued to reveal great insights on the Atonement during this time.

Clarification on Forgiveness for Sin Through Repentance

One essential doctrine that the Lord clarified through Joseph Smith was which sins will be forgiven and which will not. In the KJV, Jesus Christ taught, "All manner of sin and blasphemy shall be forgiven unto men, but the blasphemy against the Holy Ghost shall not be forgiven unto men" (Matthew 12:31). This verse intimated that all sins short of denying the Holy Ghost will eventually be forgiven. The JST made an important change—that forgiveness is possible to all "who receive [the Savior] and repent" (JST Matthew 12:31).

The JST also adds a question from the scribes: "Master, it is written that, Every sin shall be forgiven; but ye say, Whosoever speaketh against the Holy Ghost shall not be forgiven. And they asked him, saying, How can these things be?" (JST Matthew 12:43). The first question one might ask is *where* is it written that every sin will be forgiven. [133] There is no such identifiable passage in our modern Bible. Also, nowhere in the Old Testament is a sin listed as unforgivable. Some transgressions have extremely stiff penalties, including death, but forgiveness is possible. It is not consistent with the revelations given through Joseph Smith that sins can be forgiven without repentance. It seems that the scribes had misinterpreted scripture. The truly repentant can be forgiven of everything short of denying the Holy Ghost. [134]

The Lord clarified this concept further through revelations given to Joseph Smith in the last few months of 1831, found in the Gospel of Mark:

> *And then came certain men unto him, accusing him, saying, Why do ye receive sinners, seeing thou makest thyself the Son of God. But he answered them and said,* Verily I say unto you, All sins *which men have committed, when they repent,* shall be forgiven *them; for I came to preach repentance* unto the sons of men. And blasphemies wherewith soever they shall blaspheme *shall be forgiven them that come unto me and do the works which they see me do."* (JST Mark 3:28; italics indicate JST changes)

The JST gives Christ's words a context and mentions that some understood that Jesus Christ clearly taught that He was the Son of God. Here, the Savior also boldly declares that He came to preach repentance. The KJV of this verse omits that entire purpose. The Atonement does not give free repentance; it does make forgiveness possible for all who repent and do Christ-like works.

Joseph Smith later taught, "All sins shall be forgiven, except the sin against the Holy Ghost; for Jesus will save all except the sons of perdition." [135] He also made a connection with the doctrine of denying the Holy Ghost and those who killed Christ:

> *After a man has sinned against the Holy Ghost, there is no repentance for him. He has got to say that the sun does not shine while he sees it; he has got to deny Jesus Christ when the heavens have been opened unto him, and to deny the plan of salvation with his eyes open to the truth of it; and from that time he begins to be an enemy . . . When a man begins to be an enemy to this work, he hunts me, he seeks to kill me, and never ceases to thirst for my blood. He gets the spirit of the devil—the same spirit that they had who crucified the Lord of Life—the same spirit that sins against the Holy Ghost.* [136]

The JST Defines the Lord's Teaching to "Take Up Your Cross"

On several occasions in the New Testament, Jesus Christ used the phrase "take up your cross" (see Matthew 10:38; 16:24; Mark 8:34; 10:21; Luke 9:23; 14:27). To the modern reader, this clearly evokes imagery of the Atonement. With this saying, the Savior taught that to take up your cross not only necessary to be to be His disciple, but that is has to be done daily. When the young rich man was instructed to give up all his possessions, the Lord told him to take up his cross. Deducing from that situation, to take up one's cross is usually not what mankind naturally wants to do. However, the phrase was left somewhat ambiguous in the Bible. In the Book of Mormon, the Savior gave a partial definition. He taught against immorality, lustful thoughts, murder, and anger, and then stated that to "deny yourselves of these things," was to "take up your cross" (3 Nephi 12:30).

Jesus Christ revealed a more complete definition through the Prophet Joseph Smith. In the JST the Savior taught, "And now for a man to take up his cross, is to deny himself all ungodliness, and every wordly lust, and keep my commandments. Break not my commandments for to save your lives" (JST Matthew 16:24).[137] According to the JST, the cross is a symbol of suppressing personal desires and exercising obedience. Jesus Christ literally carried His cross. He struggled under the heavy tool of His own execution. This chore was after His agony in Gethsemane, and after being scourged. The wood must have torn His open wounds. The Redeemer carried His cross until He physically was no longer capable. He died on that same beam. The way Jesus Christ took up His cross exemplified the definition He gave. To forego the trial and deny the salvation of mankind would be ungodly. A worldly lust would have cried for Him to deliver Himself from the pain and extreme public ridicule. To bear His cross, was part of the Father's commands. Jesus Christ would not disobey to save His own life.

It is also interesting that Jesus Christ used this phrase "take up your cross" before He was crucified. The JST reveals that prophets had known of His crucifixion since the time of Enoch. Whether or not the disciples listening understood that the Savior would literally and physically exemplify His teaching is not clear.[138] However, when Jesus Christ was crucified it would have been a vivid and poignant reminder for them to take up their crosses.

Joseph Smith had already recorded similar teaching in a revelation to Joseph Knight in April of 1830. The Lord commanded, "you must take up your cross" (D&C 23:6). In this case, Knight needed to do something foreboding to Him, just as the Savior to a greater level took on the infinitely difficult. Knight needed to be willing to pray in all places, even "before the world" (D&C 23:6). Later, in June of 1831, the Prophet recorded, "And he that will not take up his cross and follow me, and keep my commandments, the same shall not be saved" (D&C 56:2).[139] Jesus Christ used His personal agony to motivate others to do what intimidated them.

The JST added further Atonement imagery: "forsake the world, and save your souls" (JST Matthew 16:26). It is interesting that probably within a month of this JST change, Joseph Smith received a similar statement through revelation.[140] The Lord told Sidney Gilbert, "Behold, I, the Lord, who was crucified for the sins of the world give unto you a commandment that you shall forsake the world" (D&C 53:2). The Lord used His Crucifixion to qualify Himself to ask another to forsake the world. Jesus Christ forsook the world, and allowed all mankind to be saved. As men and women forsake the world, their souls will be saved.

The JST Made Changes to the New Testament Account of the Sacrament

Jesus Christ used profound imagery to teach of His Atonement through the ordinance of the sacrament. The JST makes significant additions to the New Testament sacrament story, such as changing the order of Jesus Christ's actions to first breaking the bread and then blessing it (see JST Matthew 26:26). Also in the JST, the Savior did not teach that the bread was his body and that the wine was his blood, but that they were symbols to remember his body and blood (see JST Matthew 26:26, 28).

The Redeemer also clearly taught in the JST that He would give his body as "a ransom for you" (JST Matthew 26:26). The word "ransom" is only used a dozen or so times in the Bible. A brief summary of these other biblical teachings is helpful. In the law, in some circumstances, a guilty man could save his life by paying a ransom (see Exodus 21:30). Every man numbered among the Children of Israel was commanded to give "a ransom for his soul unto the Lord" (Exodus 30:12). Those that are ransomed are referred to as those who will have everlasting joy (see Isaiah 35:10). The Children of Israel who crossed the Red Sea on dry ground were referred to as ransomed (Isaiah 51:10). The Lord even prophesied through Hosea, "I will ransom them from the power of the grave" (Hosea 13:14). However, of the recorded words of Jesus Christ in mortality, He spoke the word only one other time. He taught that He would give His life as "a ransom for many" (see Matthew 20:28; Mark 10:45). It is a perfect word to describe the Atonement. The Lord paid the price to set others free. [141]

In the KJV account of the sacrament, the Savior taught that He would shed his blood "for many for the remission of sins" (Matthew 26:28). The word "many" in this verse intimated that perhaps Jesus Christ would not shed His blood for all. In the JST, the Savior taught that He would shed His blood for "*as* many *as shall believe on my name, for the* remission of sins" (JST Matthew 26:28; italics indicate JST changes). Perhaps these phrases are misleading if not viewed in context. The Lord had already revealed that He "suffereth the pains of all men, yea, the pains of every living creature, both men, women, and children, who belong to the family of Adam" (2 Nephi 9:21; see also D&C 18:11). There was no quota or limit; Jesus Christ suffered for all. Therefore, why would the Savior teach that He would shed his blood for "many" and "as many as shall believe on my name"? Perhaps Jesus Christ's audience is a key to further understanding. Perhaps on this occasion, He did not speak about all the ways that His Atonement would affect humanity, but how it would affect those worthy of partaking of the sacrament, as He and the Apostles were then doing. For those who repent and partake of the sacrament, or in the Savior's words "as many as shall believe in my name" will have the great blessing of "the remission of sins."

In the KJV, at the conclusion of the sacrament, Jesus Christ said to his disciples, "this do in remembrance of me" (Luke 22:19). The JST makes the Lord's words even stronger and more specific: "And I give unto you a commandment, that ye shall observe to do the things which ye have seen me do, and bear record of me even unto the end" (JST Matthew 26:29). The immediate context of this verse was the practice of observing the sacrament. Later, the JST adds the Savior's words to Mark, "for as oft as ye do this ye will remember this hour that I was with you" (JST Mark 14:22). Only in the JST did the Savior convey the same message as He blessed and passed the wine (see JST Mark 14:24). Every future sacrament would be a powerful personal experience for the Apostles, a chance to remember these touching final hours with their Savior.

The Last Supper was definitely an emotional experience. Jesus Christ told the Apostles that this would be the last time they would drink the wine together.[142] In the JST, it appears as though to some degree they understood; "And now they were grieved, and wept over him" (JST Mark 14:25).

The Lord inspired Joseph Smith to make these changes to the sacrament account in Matthew probably just before June 19, 1831.[143] In August of 1831, the Prophet recorded when and why the sacrament should be observed:

> *And that thou mayest more fully keep thyself unspotted from the world, thou shalt go to the house of prayer and offer up thy sacraments upon my holy day; for verily this is a day appointed unto you to rest from your labors, and to pay thy devotions unto the Most High.* (D&C 59:9–10)

REVELATIONS ABOUT THE ATONEMENT APRIL–JULY 1831

1. Revelation clarified that Jesus Christ taught that forgiveness is always dependent on repentance.

2. The JST defined the teaching "take up your cross" as to deny ungodliness, worldly lusts, and to keep the commandments even when one doesn't particularly want to.

3. In the JST, the Savior taught specifically of the Atonement in conjunction with the sacrament, commanded the Apostles to continue to practice the ordinance, and the Apostles wept over their Savior during this emotional experience.

August 1831

In August of 1831, Joseph Smith received six revelations that are now in the Doctrine and Covenants (see D&C 58–62). Many Saints traveled to Missouri. Hardship continued. Joseph Smith wrote, "On the 7th, I attended the funeral of sister Polly Knight . . . This was the first death in the Church in this land, and I can say, a worthy member sleeps in Jesus till the resurrection." [144] The doctrine of the Atonement was real and applicable to Saints as always. Joseph Smith paused in his translation of the Bible.

The Lord Will Remember
Sins No More

On August 1, 1831, Joseph Smith recorded a revelation in which the Lord urged His people five different times to repent (see D&C 58:15, 39, 41, 47, 48). With these cries for repentance, the Savior also taught a very comforting doctrine: "Behold, he who has repented of his sins, the same is forgiven, and I the Lord, remember them no more" (D&C 58:42). There are many verses that illustrate the power of repentance. By some counts, there are only two biblical verses that directly teach that the Lord will forget mankind's sins (see Isaiah 43:25; Jeremiah 31:34). This revelation confirmed that doctrine. It is a powerful commentary on the Savior that He not only forgives, but also is willing to forget the sins for which He suffered and bled. [145]

Intertwined in the complex tapestry of doctrine revealed in the first few years of the organized Church is a powerful story of personal application of the Atonement. The revelations made clear that Joseph Smith himself was not exempt from the need for repentance. A revelation instructed Joseph in July of 1828, "because of transgression, if thou art not aware thou wilt fall" (D&C 3:9). At this point in history, Joseph had "feared man more than God" and lost 116 pages of the Book of Mormon (D&C 3:7). In March of the next year, Joseph received a reminder of further sins, "And now I command you, my servant Joseph, to repent and walk more uprightly before me, and to yield to the persuasions of men no more" (D&C 5:21). In July of 1830, the Prophet recorded that He was "called and chosen," but "not excusable in [his] transgressions" (D&C 24:1–2). Joseph was commanded to "sin no more" (D&C 24:2). A few months later, Joseph Smith received the Lord's forgiveness, "at this time your sins are forgiven you . . . remember to sin no more" (D&C 29:3). Joseph knew from Christ Himself that he was forgiven.

Joseph Smith recorded revelations that also mentioned others' personal faults and commanded them to repent. Additionally, the Lord revealed through the Prophet to several Saints such as Emma Smith, Thomas B. Marsh, Edward Partridge, Isaac Morley, and William McLellin that they were forgiven of their sins (see D&C 25:3; 31:5; 36:1; 50:39; 64:16; 75:8). The Lord also tutored His people in general and forgave them (see D&C 29:3; 50:36; 61:2; 62:3). Revelations in the Doctrine and Covenants taught the Church to use the Atonement of Jesus Christ, that He might remember their sins no more.

Jesus Christ Can Succor Those Who Are Tempted

Also in August of 1831, Joseph Smith recorded that Jesus Christ would not only help in the process of repentance, but also in resisting temptation. This added to earlier revelations about the Redeemer's role as advocate. The revelation taught: "Jesus Christ, your advocate, . . . knoweth the weakness of man and how to succor them who are tempted" (D&C 62:1). Though the Redeemer was sinless, through the Atonement He came to know "the weakness of man." He knows what it feels like to be tempted, and testified that He will succor, or aid, those in temptation. Joseph Smith later taught,

> *The devil cannot compel mankind to evil, all was voluntary.—*
> *Those who resist the spirit of God, are liable to be led into temp-*
> *tation, and then the association of heaven is withdrawn from*
> *those who refuse to be made partakers of such great glory—God*
> *would not exert any compulsory means and the Devil could not*
> *. . . but Christ subjected the same in hope. . . . we look forward*
> *with hope, (because 'we are subjected in hope') to the time of*
> *our deliverance.* [146]

All Living Things Will Resurrect

The Lord revealed to Joseph Smith a significant doctrine about the Resurrection in the midst of these teachings. A revelation, which is now Doctrine and Covenants sixty-three, testified that "old things shall pass away, and all things become new" (D&C 63:49). This did not limit the resurrection to all mankind; it read "all things." Seven months later, the Doctrine and Covenants returned to this concept. It testifies that the Savior "saves all the works of his hands, except those sons of perdition" (D&C 76:43). This statement broadened the saving power of the Atonement even more. Jesus Christ redeemed all that He made and all that fell, including the animals and plants.

Revelation built on this concept the following month, in March of 1832. As Joseph Smith asked about the glorified beasts that John the Revelator saw in God's presence, the Lord clarified that animals will be saved (see D&C 77:2). Joseph Smith later wrote,

> John saw the actual beast in heaven, showing to John that beasts did actually exist there. . . . John saw curious looking beasts in heaven, he saw every creature that was in heaven—all the beasts, fowls, and fish in heaven—actually there, giving glory to God. . . . I suppose John saw beings there of a thousand forms, that had been saved from ten thousand times ten thousand earths like this. . . . John learned that God glorified Himself by saving all that His hands had made, whether beasts, fowls, fishes or men; and He will glorify Himself with them. . . . The four beasts were four of the most noble animals that had filled the measure of their creation, and had been saved from other worlds, because they were perfect. [147]

Joseph Smith also recorded that the Lord would "sanctify the earth, and complete the salvation of man, and judge all things, and shall redeem all things, except that which he hath not put into his power" (D&C 77:12). Jesus Christ will save and make all his creations live again.

REVELATIONS ABOUT THE ATONEMENT AUGUST 1831

1. The Lord forgets mankind's sins when they confess and forsake them.

2. Jesus Christ can succor those who are tempted.

3. All living things will resurrect.

$\mathcal{S}$eptember–$\mathcal{N}$ovember 1831

Joseph Smith recorded that from early September "til the forepart of October, I did little more than prepare to re-commence the translation of the Bible."[148] He had paused in the translation to move to Hiram, Ohio. From the end of September through November, Joseph Smith made additions and corrections from Matthew 26:1 to Mark 9:1.[149] During these three months, Joseph Smith also received nine revelations that are now part of the Doctrine and Covenants (see D&C 1; 64–70; 133). By November, Joseph Smith was working hard preparing his previously received revelations for publication in the Book of Commandments.

The JST Confirmed Jeremiah's Prophecy Regarding Judas' Blood Money

During the fall of 1831, the JST confirmed a truth originally recorded by Matthew. After Judas discarded his blood money, the chief priests didn't know what to do with it. The heartless condemners were suddenly concerned about the law and refused to put the money in the temple treasury, so they bought a potter's field. Matthew wrote that this act was a fulfillment of Jeremy's (or Jeremiah's) prophecy (see Matthew 27:9). Interestingly, the KJV book of Jeremiah contains no such prophecy.[150] There is one found in Zecharaiah 11:12–13. John Wesley wrote about this scripture, "The word 'Jeremy,' which was added to the text in later copies and thence received into many translations, is evidently a mistake; for he who spoke what Matthew here cites, or rather paraphrases, was not Jeremiah, but Zechariah."[151] The JST, however, did not change Matthew's claim. In fact, the JST confirmed it. It added another statement that buying the potter's field was prophesied, "by the mouth of Jeremy" (JST Matthew 27:10). This is yet another testimony that the Apostles must have had more scriptures available to them which testified of Jesus Christ's Atonement and the facts surrounding it.

Pilate Received A Stronger Testimony That Jesus Christ Was Innocent and Was the King of the Jews

Betrayed for thirty pieces of silver, Jesus Christ was condemned by the Jewish council. They then brought Him before Pilate. The Roman procurator questioned the Savior asking, "art thou the King of the Jews?" (Matthew 27:11). In the KJV, Jesus Christ responded, "Thou sayest" (Matthew 27:11). This statement intimated that Jesus neither confirmed nor denied the royal title. However, the JST added, "Thou sayest truly; for thus it is written of me" (JST Matthew 27:11).[152] The JST changed Jesus Christ's response to a carefully worded confession that He was the King of the Jews, and that others had already given Him this title in writing. The Savior could have been referring to such scriptures as 1 Samuel 12:12, Psalm 89:18, Isaiah 43:15, and Isaiah 44:6. However, this would be an interesting occasion for such a statement. The Redeemer was in a hearing trial before the Roman ruler, whose knowledge of the scriptures is unknown. Jesus Christ's Jewish accusers, well versed in the scriptures, would not go into the judgment hall (see John 18:28). Perhaps the Savior was not referring to scripture, but a written accusation against Him. Whatever the case, the Lord admitted to Pilate that He was, in fact, the King of the Jews.

Pilate's wife counseled with Pilate about Jesus Christ. In the JST, it clarifies that she did not have a dream, but a vision (see Matthew 27:19). This caused her to testify of the Savior's innocence and plead with her husband to leave Jesus alone.

Pilate did not listen. He turned the Savior over to the Jewish crowd. However, the JST adds that after Pilate washed his hands of Jesus Christ's blood, he urged the crowd to "do nothing unto him" (JST Matthew 27:24). The JST also harmonizes the accounts of the words Pilate wrote over the cross in Matthew with those in Luke and John (see JST Matthew 27:37; JST Mark 15:26; Luke 23:38; John 19:19–22). These verses intimate that Pilate either believed that Jesus Christ was in fact the King of the Jews or created the sign posted on the cross for cynical purposes.

The JST Changed Details in Events Regarding the Crucifixion and the Resurrection

Jesus Christ was sentenced to crucifixion at Golgotha, which the JST changed from "place of a skull" to a place of "burial" (Matthew 27:33; Mark 15:22; John 19:17; JST Matthew 27:33; JST Mark 15:22; JST John 19:17).[153] During the long agony of His crucifixion, the Savior spoke with two thieves. The JST of both Matthew 27:44 and Mark 15:32 bring the story into harmony with the account of the thieves found in Luke. Only one of the thieves spoke against the Savior, while the other defended Him. The JST changes a few of the words spoken by the defending thief in Matthew, who testified, "this man [Jesus Christ] is just, and hath not sinned" (JST Matthew 27:44). This is interesting because the thief defended Jesus Christ's righteousness, not His ability to keep Roman law. In Luke's account, the thief "said unto Jesus, Lord, remember me when thou comest into thy kingdom" (Luke 23:42). The thief makes a different request in the JST of Matthew 27:44: "he cried unto the Lord that he would save him." Whether this has reference to being saved from the cross and death, or of a hope for eternal salvation, it is unclear. Either way, the thief believed in the Savior.

The JST adds to Matthew the same answer the Lord gave to the thief in Luke's account, "This day thou shalt be with me in paradise" (JST Matthew 27:44). Years later, Joseph Smith taught more about these words the Savior said on the cross:

> I will say something about the spirits in prison. There has been much said by modern divines about the words of Jesus (when on the cross) to the thief, saying, 'This day shalt thou be with me in paradise.' King James' translators make it out to say paradise. But what is paradise? It is a modern word: it does not answer at all to the original word that Jesus made us of. Find the original of the word paradise. You may as easily find a needle in a haymow. Here is a chance for battle, ye learned men. There is nothing in the original word in Greek from which this was taken that signifies paradise; but it was—This day thou shalt be with me in the world of spirits: then I will teach you all about it and answer your inquiries. And Peter says he went and preached to the world of spirits (spirits in prison 1 Peter, 3rd chap. 19th verse), so that they who would receive it could have it answered by proxy by those who live on the earth, etc. [154]

Early on the Sunday morning following the Crucifixion, Mary Magdalene, and James' mother Mary visited Jesus Christ's tomb. There they found an "angel," "a young man . . . clothed in a long white garment," or "two men . . . in shining garments" depending on which of the Gospels is read (Matthew 28:2; Mark 16:5; Luke 24:4). The JST changed them all to read that two angels rolled back the stone, sat upon it, and testified to these two women that the Savior had risen (see JST Matthew 28:2, 5; JST Mark 16:4, 6; JST Luke 24:2, 5; JST John 20:1).

The Saints Resurrected at the Resurrection of Jesus Christ

Jesus Christ died on the cross and then rose from the grave. Thus the first resurrection began. Others resurrected after Him. Matthew 27:52 reads, "the graves were opened: and many bodies of the saints which slept arose."[155] The JST teaches this a little differently. It reads, "the graves were opened; and the bodies of the saints which slept arose, who were many" (JST Matthew 27:52). This change intimates that *all* of the Saints that had died from Adam to the days of the Savior arose at that time. Years after translating the Bible, Joseph Smith confirmed this notion by teaching the following, "We read that many bodies of the Saints arose at Christ's resurrection, probably all the saints."[156]

In November of 1831, soon after Joseph Smith made these changes, he recorded a revelation that gave specific examples of those who were with Jesus Christ when He resurrected, and perhaps even resurrected with Him: "Enoch . . . and they who were with him; the prophets who were before him; and Noah also, and they who were before him; and Moses also, and they who were before him; and from Moses to Elijah, and from Elijah to John, . . . were with Christ in his resurrection" (D&C 133:54–55). The revelation then taught that in a similar fashion all the righteous that died since the time of the Savior will resurrect when Jesus Christ comes again (see D&C 133:56).

REVELATIONS ABOUT THE ATONEMENT SEPTEMBER–NOVEMBER 1831

1. Jeremiah prophesied more about the Atonement and the facts surrounding it than are recorded in the KJV, particularly regarding what the chief priests would do with the money they used to bribe Judas to betray the Savior.

2. Pilate received stronger testimony that Jesus was innocent and truly the King of the Jews than is recorded in the KJV.

3. The JST corrected details regarding the Crucifixion and Resurrection, such as: the fact that Golgotha was a place of burial, that one of the two thieves hanging with Jesus defended the Savior's righteousness and asked the Lord to save him, that the Lord promised to teach that same thief in the world of the spirits, and that Mary Magdalene and other women found two angels testifying that the Savior had resurrected the Sunday morning after His Crucifixion.

4. Joseph Smith recorded that all the Saints from Adam to Jesus Christ's time resurrected soon after the Savior.

December 1831

Joseph Smith wrote, "After Oliver Cowdery and John Whitmer had departed for Jackson county, Missouri [delivering revelations to be printed as the Book of Commandments], I resumed the translation of the Scriptures, and continued to labor in this branch of my calling with Elder Sidney Rigdon as my scribe." [157] Joseph Smith worked with thirty-six chapters from the end of November of 1831 to February 16, 1832 (Mark 9–John 5).[158] His speed and regularity in the work is unknown. However, in order to continue discussion on these changes by month and year, the first half (Mark 9–Luke 10) of these chapters will be discussed here, and the second in the year 1832. Joseph Smith also received two revelations that are now part of the Doctrine and Covenants during this time (see D&C 71–72).

The Atonement Was Prophesied of on the Mount of Transfiguration

In the New Testament, Peter, James, and John saw Jesus Christ glorified and met Elias and Moses. In August of 1831, just a few months before this portion of the translation, the Lord revealed to Joseph Smith that "ye have not yet received" the whole account of what occurred on the Mount of Transfiguration (D&C 63:21). Based on this revelation, the New Testament only included a portion of what happened. As Joseph Smith went through the story in the process of translation, he must have been especially sensitive to revelation on the event. He knew there was more to know.

In the existing biblical account, Luke taught that Elias and Moses appeared and spoke to Jesus Christ while Peter, James, and John were sleeping (see Luke 9:32). Luke also taught that the two ancient prophets spoke to Jesus Christ about His "decease" (Luke 9:31). The JST adds that Moses and Elias spoke to the Savior about His "death and also his resurrection" (JST Luke 9:31). It was not just a somber discussion about the Savior's death, but of the glorious completion of the Atonement. They encouraged Him in His role as Savior.

The JST also revealed that John the Baptist was present on the Mount of Transfiguration (see JST Mark 9:4). What John said and did is unclear. He was not yet resurrected, for Jesus Christ had not yet been resurrected and would be the first. However, it is interesting to note that the Lord had revealed in the month before that John, Moses, and Elijah were resurrected with Jesus Christ (see D&C 133:54–55). The resurrection would have special interest for them, as it was only months away.

The JST Explains Why God is Not the God of the Dead but of the Living

The Sadducees questioned the Savior about the resurrection. They did not believe in it. At the conclusion of one particular instance, Jesus Christ in the KJV said, "He is not the God of the dead, but the God of the living: ye therefore do greatly err" (Mark 12:27). This statement seems to be contradictory to the Savior's doctrine of resurrection. It sounds as though God simply doesn't care about the dead. The JST adds one phrase that clarified this passage, "He is . . . the God of the living; for he raiseth them up out of their graves" (JST Mark 12:27). God is the God of the living simply because He will cause all to live again. Jesus Christ was boldly correcting the Sadducees.

Insights into Judas' Betrayal of the Savior

The Savior's disciples witnessed this sermon, as well as many other moments of teaching, correction, and miracles. Judas Iscariot, of course, was one of them. He was a disheartening individual in the Atonement account. Little is known of Judas' motivation to betray the Savior. Probably at the end of 1831, the JST added to the Gospel of Mark that Judas "turned away from him [Jesus Christ] and was offended because of his words" (JST Mark 14:10). The JST also adds words the Savior said to Judas immediately before he left the upper room: "What thou doest, do quickly; but beware of innocent blood" (JST Mark 14:28). This passage confirmed the many other passages that testify of Jesus Christ's foreknowledge of Judas' betrayal. It is also significant because the Savior termed His own blood as "innocent." He was innocent of breaking Roman law, innocent of breaking the Law of Moses, and innocent of sin in general.

Joseph Smith later taught why Judas betrayed the Savior:

> From apostates the faithful have received the severest persecutions. Judas was rebuked and immediately betrayed his Lord into the hands of His enemies, because Satan entered into him. There is a superior intelligence bestowed upon such as obey the Gospel with full purpose of heart, which, if sinned against, the apostate is left naked and destitute of the Spirit of God, and his is, in truth, nigh unto cursing, and his end is to be burned. When once that light which was in them is taken from them, they become as much darkened as they were previously enlightened, and then, no marvel, if all their power should be enlisted against the truth, and they, Judas like, seek the destruction of those who were their greatest benefactors. What nearer friend on earth, or in heaven, had Judas than the Savior? And his first object was to destroy Him. Who, among all the Saints in these last days can consider himself as good as our Lord? Who is as perfect? Who is as pure? Who is as holy as He was? Are they to be found? He never transgressed or broke a commandment or law of heaven—no deceit was in His mouth, neither was guile found in His heart. And yet one that ate with Him, who had often drunk of the same cup, was the first to lift up his heel against Him. Where is one like Christ? He cannot be found on earth. Then why should His followers complain, if from those whom they once called brethren, and considered as standing in the nearest relation in the everlasting covenant they should receive persecution? From what source emanated the principle which has ever been manifested by apostates from the true Church to persecute with double diligence, and seek with double perseverance, to destroy those whom they once professed to love,

with whom they once communed, and with whom they once covenanted to strive with every power in righteousness to obtain the rest of God? Perhaps our brethren will say the same that caused Satan to seek to overthrow the kingdom of God, because he himself was evil, and God's kingdom is holy. [159]

After Judas betrayed His friend and Savior, he was guilt-stricken and panicked. Convicted by his own conscience, he returned to the chief priests with whom he had conspired and confessed, "I have sinned in that I have betrayed the innocent blood" (KJV Matthew 27:4). In the KJV, the priests retorted, "What is that to us? see thou to that" (KJV Matthew 27:4). The JST, however, changes their last sentence: "What is that to us? See thou *to it; thy sins be upon thee*" (JST Matthew 27:4; italics indicate JST changes). The chief priests in both accounts were acutely apathetic to Judas' concerns. However, did they think that Judas had sinned? There are two possibilities to this JST change. Either the priests honestly believed that condemning Jesus Christ was the just and righteous thing to do, and they were merely humoring Judas by using the same word "sin" as he did. Or, the chief priests knew that Judas had honestly sinned. Could they possibly separate his betrayal from their condemnation of the Savior? If so, they were capable of immensely creative rationalization.

At the chief priests answer, Judas threw the thirty pieces of silver he had received for his betrayal on the temple grounds "and went and hanged himself" (Matthew 27:5). In Acts 1:18, Peter seems to have recounted a different kind of death. He recorded that "falling headlong, he [Judas] burst asunder in the midst, and all his bowels gushed out." The JST clarified any confusion by adding to the Matthew account that he indeed hanged himself "on a tree. And straightway he fell down, and his bowels gushed out, and he died" (JST Matthew 27:5). Such was the end of Judas, the man who betrayed the Savior to His condemners and killers.

The Apostles Doubted the Savior in Gethsemane

While Judas met with conspirators, Jesus Christ and the rest of the Apostles went to Gethsemane. [160] There, the Savior took Peter, James, and John a little further into the garden than the other eight. The JST correction, probably made at the end of 1831, attributes the adjectives of "sore amazed" and "very heavy" not to the Savior, but to the Apostles (Mark 14:33; JST Mark 14:32). The JST also adds that then the Savior "rebuked them [Peter, James, and John]" (JST Mark 14:33). They were obviously doing something wrong. This would soon be at least partially explained. The Savior confessed how burdened He felt and asked them to watch while He spent some time alone. When Jesus Christ returned, the Apostles were sleeping. The Savior urged them to "watch ye and pray, lest ye enter into temptation" (Mark 14:38). The JST sheds new light on this situation. It adds an intriguing doubt to the Apostles, "and the disciples began . . . to complain in their hearts wondering if this be the Messiah" (JST Mark 14:32). For at least one moment, the Savior's friends and disciples were tempted to doubt that He was the Savior while He was in the very act of saving. [161]

In order to understand such a change, a few of the other changes the JST made about the Twelve Apostles are insightful. Even more of the disciples' human frailties are apparent. According to the JST of Luke 12:10, the Apostles had "spoken evil against him [Jesus Christ] before the people; for they were afraid to confess him before men." The JST of John 11:16 showed that the Apostles worried prematurely that the Savior would be killed, "for they feared lest the Jews should take Jesus and put him to death, for as yet they did not understand the power of God." Joseph Smith wrote,

> *Since the apostles fell asleep all men who profess a belief in the truth of their mission, extol their virtues and celebrate their fame. It seems to have been forgotten that they were men of infirmities and subject to all the feelings, passions, and imperfections common to other men.* [162]

The Apostles were full of faith and devotion, but they were also human with doubts and shortcomings.

Perhaps even more telling is what effect the Apostles' doubting in Gethsemane had on the Savior. The JST adds that Jesus Christ knew the doubts in His Apostles' hearts (see JST Mark 14:32). As the Redeemer began the Atonement, He was alone spiritually and emotionally, while only a stone's cast away from his sleeping friends. In the JST, Jesus Christ remained alone, waiting until after His Apostles "had finished their sleep," to wake them (JST Mark 14:42; see JST Matthew 26:46).

The Apostles Abandoned the
Savior in the Garden

The Savior awakened His Apostles when a band of men came to seize Him. Peter tried to physically defend Jesus Christ, and cut off Malchus's ear. The Redeemer miraculously healed Malchus and urged His Apostles to sheath their swords. The Savior didn't want to be defended. The JST then adds, "the disciples when they heard this saying, all forsook him and fled" (JST Mark 14:50). The disciples' retreat was at least partially motivated by Jesus Christ's words, not fear alone.

The Crowd Cried for Pilate
to Deliver Jesus

The arrest of Jesus Christ would have been big news. There was a multitude gathered when Pilate gave the people a choice to free the Savior or Barabbas. The KJV of Matthew states that Pilate "was wont" to give the people such a choice (Matthew 27:15). The JST adds to Mark that "it was common at that feast for Pilate to release unto them one prisoner" (JST Mark 15:6). If the Savior's followers knew of the custom of releasing one prisoner, surely they would try to gather in the place of voting to attempt to save Jesus Christ. It is unclear how informed they were of the proceedings, or whether or not they were allowed to enter. When Pilate asked the crowd's wishes, the JST inserts that they cried out "to deliver Jesus unto them" (JST Mark 15:8). It is also unclear whether the crowd was sympathetic and wanted the Savior's safety, or wished to inflict a hostile sentence themselves. However, the KJV then recounts, "But the chief priests moved the people, that he should rather release Barabbas unto them" (Mark 15:11).[163] Somehow, the popular vote was persuaded to cry for the Savior's crucifixion (see Mark 15:13).[164] There is no more insight available as to how the chief priests were able to successfully persuade the multitude. However, in the JST, the chief priests were even more evil and conspiring against the Savior than in the KJV.

Clarification of Simeon's Prophecy
on Jesus Christ's Death

Also during the end of 1831, Joseph Smith made changes to the book of Luke. This Gospel retold of the Savior's infancy. Simeon, an old temple worker, held the 40-day-old Savior and prophesied that He would save mankind. During Simeon's prophecy, in the KJV, he parenthetically told Mary, "Yea, a sword shall pierce through thy own soul also" (Luke 2:35). This passage, when interpreted at face value insinuated a sword would pierce both the Savior and Mary. The JST clarified this prophecy, "Yea, a spear shall pierce through him [Christ] to the wounding of thine [Mary's] own soul also" (JST Luke 2:35). Simeon specifically prophesied that Jesus Christ would be pierced by a spear, which was fulfilled as is recorded in John 19:34. The Savior's death pierced Mary emotionally as she anguished over her Son's death.

The JST Added John the Baptist's Long Quotation on the Atonement

As previously discussed, John the Baptist also testified of the Savior. At this point in the translation process, Joseph Smith made another significant addition. He had already read and made relatively few changes to the accounts in Matthew and Mark of John preaching to the people in Judea. In John's preaching, he quoted Isaiah 40:3–4. However, the JST adds to Luke 3 an entire paragraph to John's quotation testifying of the Savior:

> For behold, and lo, he [Jesus Christ] shall come, as it is written in the book of the prophets, to take away the sins of the world, and to bring salvation unto the heathen nations, to gather together those who are lost, who are of the sheepfold of Israel; Yea, even the dispersed and afflicted . . . And to be a light unto all who sit in darkness, unto the uttermost parts of the earth; to bring to pass the resurrection from the dead, and to ascend up on high, to dwell on the right hand of the Father. (JST Luke 3:5)

This quotation added to what is recorded in Isaiah. Interestingly, the JST made no correction or insertion to the Isaiah verse in the Bible. [165] Either John quoted one verse of Isaiah, elaborated on it, and then quoted the other, or the JST revealed more of Isaiah's words. Perhaps John had a more complete record. Whichever the case, John did not only teach of one greater than he, but of a Savior who would "take away sins of the world" and "bring to pass the resurrection from the dead."

REVELATIONS ABOUT THE ATONEMENT
DECEMBER 1831

1. Elijah and Moses spoke to the Savior about his Atonement on the Mount of Transfiguration.

2. Jesus taught that God is not the God of the dead but of the living, because God will raise all the dead to life.

3. The JST revealed insights into Judas' betrayal, such as his offense at Jesus Christ's teaching, the Savior's warning to Judas not to betray innocent blood, and the possibility that the chief priests thought that Judas was sinning, as well as reconciling the two accounts of Judas' death.

4. For at least one moment, the Apostles doubted if Jesus Christ was the Messiah, even as He was in the process of saving them, and Jesus Christ knew their hearts.

5. The JST revealed at least a partial reason why the Apostles abandoned the Savior in the garden.

6. When given the decision between Jesus Christ and Barabbas, the crowd first cried out for Jesus to be delivered, then were persuaded to ask for Barabbas' release.

7. Revelation clarified Simeon's prophecy of Jesus Christ's death.

8. John the Baptist either used Isaiah's prophecy as a resource in his own prophetic teaching on the Atonement, or he quoted an unrecorded prophecy by Isaiah on the subject.

Chapter 5

REVELATIONS ABOUT THE
ATONEMENT IN 1832

In 1832, the church had its two-year anniversary. Joseph Smith continued his work with the Bible, and continued to receive other revelations. He had already recorded many great doctrines about the Atonement. However, one of the most enlightening would be revealed in 1832, in direct connection with the JST. It changed the theology of The Church of Jesus Christ of Latter-day Saints dramatically. It enlarged man's understanding of the ramifications of the Atonement.

*J*anuary 1832

In December 1831, Joseph Smith paused in his translation of the Bible and traveled with Sidney Rigdon to Kirtland Ohio. The Prophet wrote, "For this time until the 8th or 10th of January, 1832, myself and Elder Rigdon continued to preach in Shalersville, Ravenna, and other places, setting forth the truth, vindicating the cause of our Redeemer." [166] Joseph Smith actively taught about Jesus Christ and his work during this time of revelation. On January 10, the Prophet received a revelation declaring, "it is expedient to translate again" (D&C 73:3). Joseph Smith then recorded, "Upon the reception of the foregoing word of the Lord, I recommenced the translation of the Scriptures, and labored diligently until just before the conference, which was to convene on the 25th of January."[167] Further work on the New Testament yielded a previously unrevealed truth about the Savior during His Crucifixion.

Jesus Christ Forgave His Roman Crucifiers While on the Cross

The JST made a clarifying change to the Savior's words on the cross in Luke's Gospel. In the KJV, Jesus Christ said, "Father, forgive them; for they know not what they do" (Luke 23:34). It appears as though Jesus Christ forgave the very unrepentant sinners who cried for His blood. This is inconsistent with some of the Redeemer's previously discussed teachings that mankind had to repent to receive forgiveness. The JST clarified what the Savior spoke, adding the phrase, "Meaning the soldiers who crucified him" (JST Luke 23:34). Jesus Christ maintained his superhuman compassion even through torture. He pled that the Father would forgive the naïve Roman soldiers. However, Jesus Christ did not ask for the Jews' forgiveness without requiring their repentance.

The JST Clarified John's Testimony of the Savior

The JST also shed light on John's understanding of the Savior. The first verse of John as found in the KJV states, "in the beginning was the Word, and the Word was with God, and the Word was God." The JST clarifies Jesus Christ's role in this verse: "In the beginning was the gospel preached through the Son. And the gospel was the word, and the word was with the Son, and the Son was with God, and the Son was of God" (JST John 1:1). Several verses later the JST also adds, "For in the beginning was the Word, even the Son, who is made flesh, and sent unto us by the will of the Father" (JST John 1:16). These verses spoke of the premortal Savior, that His gospel was preached through Him then, and that He came to the earth in obedience to the Father. Three concepts validate this conclusion. First, John's two statements began with "in the beginning." Second, John's next subject was the Creation, and the JST clarifies that Jesus Christ is the Creator (John 1:3; JST John 1:10). After introducing the fact that John the Baptist would testify of these things, this chapter then testifies of the Savior's birth (see John 1:14; JST John 1:13). It appears to be a chronological procession from pre-mortal life, to the Creation, to Jesus Christ's birth.

Third, also in this chapter, and directly before one of the verses in question, John the Baptist proclaimed that the Redeemer was "before" him (John 1:15). John was born before the Savior; therefore he must be referring to a time before Jesus Christ's birth. The Redeemer was qualified to perform the Atonement because He was chosen "in the beginning."

In the JST, John's testimony that Jesus Christ was literally the Son of God is clearer and more frequently stated. The first eighteen verses of John in the KJV use the phrases "only begotten of the Father" and "the only begotten Son" to describe Jesus Christ (see John 1:14; 1:18). Though these phrases clearly state the Savior's divine ancestry, the JST gives Jesus Christ the title of "the Son" an additional eight times in those verses (see JST John 1:1, 7, 10, 16, 18). The JST testifies of Jesus Christ's divine Sonship in several other changes, and elaborated on its importance. [168] Later in John, the JST adds Jesus Christ's words, "For I can of mine own self do nothing" to the sentence "because I seek not mine own will, but the will of the Father which hath sent me" (JST John 5:30; KJV John 5:30). The JST further highlights the fact that Jesus Christ was the literal Son of God, and that His completion of the Atonement was in obedience and submission to His divine Father.

REVELATIONS ABOUT THE ATONEMENT JANUARY 1832

1. Jesus Christ asked the Father to forgive his Roman crucifiers while He was on the cross, not the unrepentant Jewish leaders who put him to death.

2. Revelation clarified John's testimony in John 1 that he believed Jesus Christ was chosen premortally and His gospel was preached before He created the earth, and that Jesus Christ was literally the Son of God.

February 1832

In February of 1832, Joseph Smith received one of the most extraordinary revelations of this dispensation. The Prophet wrote, "Upon my return from Amherst conference, I resumed the translation of the Scriptures. From sundry revelations which had been received, it was apparent that many important points touching the salvation of man, had been taken from the Bible, or lost before it was compiled. It appeared self-evident from what truths were left, that if God rewarded every one according to the deeds done in the body the term 'Heaven,' as intended for the Saints' eternal home must include more kingdoms than one. Accordingly, on the 16th of February, 1832, while translating St. John's Gospel, myself and Elder Rigdon saw the following vision."[169] Joseph Smith then recorded what is now Doctrine and Covenants seventy-six.

Joseph Smith and Sidney Rigdon saw this vision or visions in an upstairs room of the John Johnson farmhouse in Hiram, Ohio. Philo Dibble, who was present, related the following:

> *During the time that Joseph and Sidney were in the spirit and saw the heavens open, there were other men in the room, perhaps twelve, among whom I was one during a part of the time—probably two-thirds of the time,—I saw the glory and felt the power, but did not see the vision. . . .*
>
> *Joseph would, at intervals, say: "What do I see?" as one might say while looking out the window and beholding what all in the room could not see. Then he would relate what he had seen or what he was looking at. Then Sidney replied, "I see the same." Presently Sidney would say, "what do I see?" and would repeat what he had seen or was seeing, and Joseph would reply, "I see the same."*
>
> *This manner of conversation was repeated at short intervals to the end of the vision, and during the whole time not a word was spoken by any other person. Not a sound nor motion made by anyone but Joseph and Sidney, and it seemed to me that they never moved a joint or limb during the time I was there, which I think was over an hour, and to the end of the vision.*
>
> *Joseph sat firmly and calmly at the time in the midst of a magnificent glory, but Sidney sat limp and pale, apparently as limber as a rag, observing which, Joseph remarked, smilingly, "Sidney is not used to it as I am."*[170]

This vision revealed the ramifications of a first and second resurrection. It revealed that mankind was not destined to go to merely a heaven or a hell, but to differing degrees of glory. Joseph Smith wrote about this revelation,

> *Nothing could be more pleasing to the Saints upon the order of the kingdom of the Lord, than the light which burst upon the world through the foregoing vision. Every law, every commandment, every promise, every truth, and every point touching the destiny of man, from Genesis to Revelation, where the purity of the scriptures remain unsullied by the folly of men, go to show the perfection of the theory and witnesses the fact that that document is a transcript from the records of the eternal world. The sublimity of the ideas; the purity of the language; the scope for action; the continued duration for completion, in order that the heirs of salvation may confess the Lord and bow the knee; the rewards for faithfulness, and the punishments for sins, are so much beyond the narrow-mindedness of men, that every honest man is constrained to exclaim: "It came from God."* [171]

The Subject of the Resurrection Brought about the Revelation

While translating chapter five of the book of John on February 16, 1832, Joseph Smith felt inspired to change verse twenty-nine from describing two resurrections, one of life and the other of damnation, to become one resurrection of the "just" and one of the "unjust" (JST John 5:29). Joseph Smith then recorded, "This caused us [Joseph and Sidney Rigdon] to marvel, for it was given unto us of the Spirit. And while we meditated upon these things, the Lord touched the eyes of our understandings and they were opened" (D&C 76:18–19). Joseph Smith and Sidney Rigdon then saw the series of grand visions.

The revelation was not an addition to the New Testament text. The ancient text was the catalyst. Though the idea of two resurrections was not new, the doctrinal ramifications that followed were. It revealed the power of the Atonement over mankind in an infinitely inclusive way. It is no wonder that a verse pertaining so specifically to the resurrection would be the catalyst for such a meaningful revelation.

Joseph Smith Saw the Premortal and Resurrected Savior in Vision

Joseph Smith recorded that as part of this great vision, "our eyes were opened . . . so as to see and understand the things of God—even those things which were from the beginning before the world was, which were ordained of the Father, through his Only Begotten Son, who was in the bosom of the Father, even from the beginning" (D&C 76:12–13). Joseph Smith had recorded the account of the premortal Savior as early as the fall of 1830, however, in this instance, he saw it. The vision covered from the premortal life to man's inheritance after this life. Joseph Smith later commented, "I could explain a hundred fold more than I ever have of the glories of the kingdoms manifested to me in the vision, were I permitted, and were the people prepared to receive them." [172] Joseph Smith knew the power and implications of the Atonement by study, by revelation, and by sight.

As part of this divine vision, Joseph Smith and Sidney Rigdon saw God the Father and Jesus Christ. Joseph Smith then recorded one of the most powerful and memorable testimonies of Jesus Christ: "And now, after the many testimonies which have been given of him, this is the testimony, last of all, which we give of him: That he lives!" (D&C 76:22). No words could teach such a lesson. Joseph Smith experienced another manifestation that the Savior indeed had resurrected. Jesus Christ is the central figure of the vision, as well as mankind's degree of glory in the life to come. The Redeemer is, as the Prophet wrote, "of whom we bear record; and the record which we bear is the fulness of the gospel of Jesus Christ, who is the Son, who we saw and with whom we conversed in the heavenly vision" (D&C 76:14).

Accompanying the heavenly vision, the Prophet and Sidney Rigdon heard a "voice bearing record that he is the Only Begotten of the Father" (D&C 76:23). This is consistent with many of Jesus Christ's other appearances in scripture (see Matthew 3:17; Matthew 17:5; Joseph Smith—History 1:17). In every other case, the voice was clearly God the Father's. This vision was probably no exception.

Jesus Christ Atoned for All on Many Worlds

The divine voice also testified, "by him [Jesus Christ], through him, and of him, the worlds are and were created" (D&C 76:24). The fact that the Savior created many worlds was not new revelation. In June of 1830, the JST indicated that the Lord created "worlds without number" (Moses 1:33). However, the Lord in Doctrine and Covenants seventy-six continued, "and the inhabitants thereof are begotten sons and daughters unto God" (D&C 76:24). This verse expands the comprehensible limits of the Atonement past any previous scripture. It testifies that all of the inhabitants of these infinite worlds "are begotten [or born again] sons and daughters unto God" (D&C 76:24). The Atonement covers not just all of the people who ever lived or will ever live on earth, but also all that lived on countless other worlds. Joseph Smith confirmed this interpretation eleven years later in a poetic commentary on the vision:

> By him, of him, and through him, the worlds were all made,
> Even all that careen in the heavens so broad,
> Whose inhabitants, too, from the first to the last,
> Are sav'd by the very same Savior of ours [173]

The first verse of this recorded revelation states, "the Lord is God, and beside him there is no Savior" (D&C 76:1).[174] He was the only Savior for the entire universe.

Joseph Smith and Sidney Rigdon saw two separate groups "worshipping God, and the Lamb" (D&C 76:21). The angels were one group, and the other they described as "them who are sanctified" (D&C 76:21). In his poetic interpretation, Joseph Smith called one group "angels and hosts" and the other "sanctified beings from worlds that have been."[175] These sanctified ones were another testimony of Jesus Christ's atoning power on other worlds.

The Atonement Will Not Save
Sons of Perdition

Next, Joseph Smith and Sidney Rigdon saw Lucifer cast out from the presence of God premortally. Joseph Smith then recorded that they saw those who let themselves be overcome by Satan and denied Jesus Christ and the Holy Ghost. The voice of the vision called them "sons of perdition" and emphatically stated, "it had been better for them never to have been born" (D&C 76:32). This is simply a true statement, not dramatics. All others will progress and receive a kingdom of glory. These will not (see D&C 76:43–44).[176] The revelation states that for these sons of perditions "there is no forgiveness in this world nor in the world to come" (D&C 76:34). As was previously quoted, Joseph Smith later taught about sons of perdition,

> *All sins shall be forgiven, except the sin against the Holy Ghost; for Jesus will save all except the sons of perdition. What must a man do to commit the unpardonable sin? He must receive the Holy Ghost, have the heavens opened unto him, and know God, and then sin against Him. After a man has sinned against the Holy Ghost, there is no repentance for him. He has got to say that the sun does not shine while he sees it; he has got to deny Jesus Christ when the heavens have been opened unto him, and to deny the plan of salvation with his eyes open to the truth of it. . . . You cannot save such persons; you cannot bring them to repentance; they make open war, like the devil, and awful is the consequence.* [177]

Sons of perdition will not be made clean through the Atonement, for they "denied the Only Begotten Son of the Father, having crucified him unto themselves and put him to an open shame" (D&C 76:35). This is telling language. Joseph Smith wrote of such people, "When a man begins to be an enemy to this work, he hunts me, he seeks to kill me, and never ceases to thirst for my blood. He gets the spirit of the devil—the same spirit that they had who crucified the Lord of Life—the same spirit that sins against the Holy Ghost." [178] Sons of perdition seek the demise of the good. They would crucify the Savior again. These will not inherit any glory. They did not utilize the Atonement, but made it as though it were only a tragedy, the degrading death, or "open shame" of the Son of God.

The Atonement Will Sanctify the Earth

The revelation then testified that Jesus Christ "came into the world . . . to be crucified for the world, and to bear the sins of the world, and to sanctify the world, and to cleanse it from all unrighteousness" (D&C 76:41). This statement appears to not include any new doctrine, but is a sentence of stirring testimony. Joseph Smith later wrote, "the world and earth are not synonymous terms. The world is the human family." [179] Earth is the planet the Lord created. Based on this teaching, the revelation referred only to the human family. However, after clarifying the difference between the terms earth and world, the Prophet wrote in his poetic interpretation of this verse that the Atonement would "sanctify earth for a blessed repose." [180] Earlier revelation taught that the earth was alive and begged to be cleansed. The Atonement will cleanse even the earth itself, redeeming it from the Fall, and allowing it to return to God's presence. In fact, the very next month, March 1832, Joseph Smith asked the Lord questions about the John's visions in the book of Revelation. In response, the Prophet received a revelation teaching that the earth would be changed into a "sanctified, immortal, and eternal state" and described as a "sea of glass" in Revelation 4:6 (D&C 77:1).

In December of the same year, Joseph Smith recorded that the earth

> must needs be sanctified from all unrighteousness, that it may be prepared for the celestial glory; for after it hath filled the measure of its creation, it shall be crowned with glory, even with the presence of God the Father; that bodies who are of the celestial kingdom may possess it forever and ever; for, for this intent was it made and created . . . the earth abideth the law of a celestial kingdom, for it filleth the measure of its creation, and transgresseth not the law—wherefore, it shall be sanctified; yea, notwithstanding it shall die, it shall be quickened again, and shall abide the power by which it is quickened and the righteous shall inherit it. (D&C 88:18–20, 25–26)

Because of the Fall, the earth shall die and pass away just like Adam and Eve. However, also like them, it shall be exalted to celestial glory.

The Great Majority of the Father's Children Will Inherit Glory

In this revelation, the Lord revealed through Joseph Smith that the sons of perdition would be "the only ones on whom the second death shall have any power" (D&C 76:37). The revelation repeated in similar language, even "the only ones who shall not be redeemed in the due time of the Lord, after the sufferings of his wrath" (D&C 76:38). By logical deduction, these verses teach that all others would overcome the second death, and would be redeemed. All humanity would be saved from death and hell except for the sons of perdition. In fact, "all the rest shall be brought forth by the resurrection of the dead, through the triumph and the glory of the Lamb" (D&C 76:39).

This idea is revolutionary to most religious thinkers. Influential religious minds of Joseph Smith's era taught nothing that resembled these three degrees of glory. They taught of only two vastly contrasting inheritances, a glorious heaven, and an eternal hell. Reverend George Whitefield taught that, "hell is no painted fire," and, "the torments reserved for the wicked hereafter are eternal. These shall go away into everlasting punishment." [181] He continued,

> *and if this be granted (and who dares deny it?) it follows, that if a wicked man dieth in his wickedness, and under the wrath of God, he must continue in that state to all eternity. For, since there is no possibility of his being delivered out of such a condition, but by and through Christ; and since, at the hour of death, the time of Christ's mediation and intercession for him is irrecoverably gone; the same reason that may be given, why God should punish a sinner that dieth under the guilt of his sins for a single day, will equally hold good, why he should continue to punish him for a year, an age, nay to all eternity.* [182]

Jonathan Edwards taught, "The everlasting flames of hell will not be thought too hot for the rebellious; and when they have there burnt through millions of ages, he [God] will not repent him of the evil which is befallen them." [183]

John Wesley taught that both reward and punishment in the afterlife are eternal. In his words, "the punishment lasts as long as the reward." [184] Alexander Campbell taught similarly,

> *We must say, in regard to destruction as involving the sanctions of the Christian religion, that salvation and damnation are its sublime, awful and tremendous sanctions. He that diminishes either of these in its character, extent or duration, detracts just so much from the claims of the whole institution upon the attention and acceptance of every man. If the life to be enjoyed is not to be everlasting, or if the condemnation to hell (for so our Lord denominates it) is to terminate in a year, a century or a millennium, then neither the salvation is of infinite importance, nor the*

condemnation of infinite dread. A pain, however intense, which
continues but a day, a year or an age, is nothing compared to a
pain that is everlasting. [185]

This doctrine of three degrees of glory illuminates God's mercy. Alexander Campbell interpreted this mercy differently. He taught, "We have reason to infer that there will be such a perfect acquiescence in his final adjudication of the whole intellectual and moral universe as to fill every pure heart with joy unspeakable and full of glory; even when that judgment may condemn to eternal anguish a relation now dear to us." [186] Jonathan Edwards used even more vivid rhetoric,

> *Is it not a terrible thing to a wretched soul, when it shall lie*
> *roaring perpetually in the flames of hell, and the God of mercy*
> *himself shall laugh at them; when they shall cry out for mercy,*
> *yea, for one drop of water, and God shall mock them instead of*
> *relieving them; when none in heaven or earth can help them but*
> *God, and he shall rejoice over them in their calamity?* [187]

Joseph Smith revealed a Lord of more mercy, and a more powerful Atonement, than any other religious thinker of the day.

This doctrine was even hard for many of Joseph Smith's followers. Though the Prophet wrote that it was pleasing to the Saints, his statement did not include all members of the Church. Brigham Young taught,

> *When God revealed to Joseph Smith and Sidney Rigdon that*
> *there was a place prepared for all, according to the light they had*
> *received and their rejection of evil and practice of good, it was a*
> *great trial to many, and some apostatized because God was not*
> *going to send to everlasting punishment heathen and infants, but*
> *had a place of salvation in due time, for all and would bless the*
> *honest and virtuous and truthful, whether they ever belonged to*
> *any church or not.* [188]

The proportion of saved souls in contrast to those in perdition will be staggering. The Lord is mighty to save and will save the vast majority of mankind. God's plan was not to send His children to earth and polarize them to either heaven or hell. He will divinely reward each child with as much glory as He can for each situation. The Atonement allows that resurrection that allows mankind to receive glory. It also enables any and all repentance in each individual's life. Jesus Christ is truly a Savior, though each individual will decide to what degree. This is not to say that sons of perdition will not resurrect, but they will be the only ones who will not resurrect with glory. Joseph Smith recorded that everyone outside of perdition, after this life, would not just go to a heaven and a hell, but to degrees of glory.

The Celestial Kingdom

Joseph Smith and Sidney Rigdon saw these degrees of glory. Joseph Smith later taught, "When any person receives a vision of Heaven, he sees things that he never thought of before." [189] This must have been the case in this instance. He also taught,

> *Salvation cannot come without revelation; it is in vain for anyone to minister without it. No man is a minister of Jesus Christ without being a Prophet. No man can be a minister of Jesus Christ except he has a testimony of Jesus; and this is the spirit of prophecy. Whenever salvation has been administered, it has been by testimony. Men at the present time testify of heaven and of hell, and have never seen either; and I will say that no man knows these things without this.* [190]

This vision separated Joseph Smith from other leaders and preachers on the subject of the afterlife. He testified that such revelation is linked to His testimony of the Savior. The Prophet first saw the highest degree of glory, or the celestial kingdom. The word "celestial" is only mentioned once outside of the Doctrine and Covenants (see 1 Corinthians 15:40). This kingdom would contain those who were baptized, kept the commandments, received the testimony of Jesus Christ, and were cleansed through the Atonement. Those in the celestial kingdom would be "just men made perfect through Jesus the mediator of the new covenant, who wrought out this perfect atonement through the shedding of his own blood" (D&C 76:69). They would come forth in the first resurrection and inherit "all things" (D&C 76:55, 59). They "shall dwell in the presence of God and his Christ forever and ever" (D&C 76:62).

This doctrine to many is inconceivable. Humanity can be made not only clean, but "perfect." The revelation described those who enter the celestial kingdom, "They are gods, even the sons of God"

(D&C 76:58). They will dwell with their Father and become what their Father is. Joseph Smith taught later, "If you wish to go whare [where] God is you must be like God."[191] Not only is the doctrine that there are degrees of glory altogether new, but also the idea that mankind, through the Atonement can become like Jesus Christ, and like the Father. In other words, the Atonement paid for everything that stands between man and God, all sin, all mortality, and all weakness. Only through Jesus Christ can man become exalted.

Those in the Celestial Kingdom Have Celestial Bodies

The Lord revealed through Joseph Smith another aspect of how those who will inherit the celestial kingdom will become like the Father. The revelation described them as "they whose bodies are celestial" (D&C 76:70). It appears as though the kingdom individuals inherit will affect their resurrected body. The revelation continues to describe those in the celestial kingdom, "whose glory is that of the sun, even the glory of God, the highest of all, whose glory the sun of the firmament is written of as being typical" (D&C 76:70). They will literally be celestial beings.

Later this same year, Joseph Smith received another revelation that confirmed this doctrine: "They who are of a celestial spirit shall receive the same body which was a natural body; even ye shall receive your bodies, and your glory shall be that glory by which your bodies are quickened. Ye who are quickened by a portion of the celestial glory shall then receive of the same, even a fulness" (D&C 88:28–29). The revelation continues to describe those in the two lower kingdoms: "And they who are quickened by a portion of the terrestrial glory shall then receive of the same, even a fulness. And also they who are quickened by a portion of the telestial glory shall then receive of the same, even a fulness" (D&C 88:30–31). The bodies of God's children will resurrect into different glories proportionate to the lives they led, and therefore, the kingdom they inherit. It appears as though this difference in resurrected bodies is what Paul taught in 1 Corinthians 15. He compared the resurrection to planting seeds. If someone plants grain, they will receive grain. If they live a celestial way, they will receive a matching glory. Paul wrote, "There are also celestial bodies, and bodies terrestrial: but the glory of the celestial is one, and the glory of the terrestrial is another" (1 Corinthians 15:40). The JST adds that there were also "bodies telestial" (JST 1 Corinthians 15:40).

Jesus Christ Was the Firstborn

The revelation taught that those who will inherit the celestial kingdom are those who truly belong to the Church of Jesus Christ, or "the church of the Firstborn" (D&C 76:54, 71, 94, 102; see also D&C 76:67). This phrase is only used once in the Bible (see Hebrews 12:23). The Doctrine and Covenants uses it ten times (see D&C 76:54, 67, 71, 94, 102; 77:11; 78:21; 88:5; 93:22; 107:19).

It is significant that Jesus Christ was described as the Firstborn. Obviously, He was not physically the firstborn on earth, but spiritually. There are a handful of biblical verses that suggest this doctrine (see Psalm 89:27, John 1:1, Romans 8:29, Colossians 1:13, Hebrews 1:6), even though biblical exegetes argue their meaning and interpretation. Previous to this point, Joseph Smith had recorded revelation on the doctrine of Jesus Christ in the premortal life, which testified that "mine Only Begotten Son . . . was with me from the beginning" (Moses 2:26). Later, the Lord revealed that mankind's spirits were not created out of nothing, but were organized intelligences (see D&C 93). There must have been an order to this spiritual birth or organization. The same revelation reported Jesus Christ's statement, "I was in the beginning with the Father, and am the Firstborn" (D&C 93:21). He is all mankind's spiritual elder brother. [192]

The fact that Jesus Christ was spiritually the Firstborn of God sheds light on the Old Testament practice of sacrificing the "firstlings of the flocks" (Moses 5:5). It was in similitude of the sacrifice of the Firstborn of God. Also, it explains the Old Testament practice of giving the firstborn male the birthright. The firstborn represented the father and was his heir. He acted for the father. The practice was a similitude of the Savior, who represents the Father, is His divine heir, and manages the household of God.

The Terrestrial Kingdom

The vision revealed that the Lord prepared a lesser kingdom than the celestial. It does not have the glory of the celestial. The voice of the vision described those in the terrestrial kingdom as those "whose glory differs from that of the church of the Firstborn who have received the fulness of the Father, even as that of the moon differs from the sun" (D&C 76:71). While those in the celestial kingdom were compared to the glory of the sun, those in the terrestrial were compared to the glory of the moon (see D&C 76:78). The Son, but not the Father, would personally visit them (see D&C 76:78). Those in this kingdom "received not the testimony of Jesus in the flesh, but afterwards received it" or were "not valiant in the testimony of Jesus" (D&C 76:74, 79). They either died without the law, or were not willing to live it. The Lord would clarify subsequently that those who died without law and would have accepted it, may inherit the celestial kingdom (see D&C 137).

The Telestial Kingdom

The telestial kingdom is the lowest kingdom of glory. All of its inhabitants "received not the gospel of Christ, neither the testimony of Jesus. They are the "liars . . . adulterers . . . whoremongers, and whosoever loves and makes a lie" (D&C 76:103). According to most religious thinkers, such vile sinners deserve and will receive eternal hell. Joseph Smith recorded that they receive glory after they are clean. They will have to suffer for their sins while others are participating in the first resurrection. They will rise again during the second. The vision taught, "They are they who shall not be redeemed from the devil until the last resurrection, until the Lord, even Christ the Lamb, shall have finished his work" (D&C 76:85; see also D&C 76:106).

Once these souls have paid for their sins, they will gain various degrees of glory. The revelation compares them to the various glories of the stars. Though it is the lowest kingdom of glory and will not be in the presence of God or of Christ, it will receive the ministration of angels. Though it is the lowest kingdom, it is still a kingdom of glory. Joseph Smith recorded that "the glory of the telestial . . . surpasses all understanding" (D&C 76:89).

REVELATIONS ABOUT THE ATONEMENT FEBRUARY 1832

1. Pondering the subject of the resurrection brought about a great vision on the resurrection and its effects on the entire human race.

2. Joseph Smith saw the premortal and resurrected Savior in vision.

3. Jesus Christ, the only Savior for the entire universe, atoned for all the souls on worlds without number.

4. The Atonement will not cleanse sons of perdition.

5. The Atonement will sanctify the earth.

6. The great majority of the Father's children will inherit a kingdom of glory.

7. Revelation described the celestial kingdom and the characteristics of those that will inherit it.

8. Those who will inherit the celestial kingdom will gain celestial bodies.

9. Jesus Christ was spiritually the Firstborn of the Father.

10. Revelation described the terrestrial kingdom and the characteristics of those that will inherit it.

11. Revelation described the telestial kingdom and the characteristics of those that will inherit it.

In Conclusion

JOSEPH SMITH BELIEVED IN AND HELD TO the principles taught in the Bible. However, he also taught, "Take away the Book of Mormon and the revelations, and where is our religion? We have none." [193] Modern revelation plays an essential role in delineating the doctrines of "Mormonism," and supplementing the biblical revelations. The revelations Joseph Smith received covered a great variety of topics: the law of consecration, gathering of Zion, temples, instructions for preaching the gospel, organization of the priesthood and their duties, etc. It is interesting to note, however, that interwoven throughout all of these various subjects, there were many insights on the Atonement. All truths of the gospel can be related to the Atonement. As Joseph Smith himself taught, and as was previously quoted,

> *The fundamental principles of our religion are the testimony of the Apostles and Prophets, concerning Jesus Christ, that He died, was buried, and rose again the third day, and ascended into heaven; and all other things which pertain to our religion are only appendages to it.* [194]

In analyzing what the Lord revealed through Joseph Smith and how it compared to other religious thought of the day, five general conclusions became apparent:

1. In only two years, the Lord revealed through Joseph Smith a flood of doctrinal knowledge that contrasts and often conflicts with many of the views of his day.

2. These revelations were part of a process that demonstrated general patterns of revelation.

3. The revelations and biblical corrections and additions heightened the attributes and divinity of the Savior, and gave further insight into many other figures involved in the events surrounding the Atonement.

4. Doctrines revealed through Joseph Smith made the Atonement immensely greater in depth and reach.

5. The Lord revealed through Joseph Smith that the Atonement has been the focus of the gospel since Adam, and even before Adam in the premortal life.

Joseph Smith Recorded a Flood of Knowledge

All of the other influential religious figures referenced in this book were well-educated. John Wesley was educated at Christ Church, Oxford University. George Whitefield was educated at Pembroke College, Oxford. Charles Finney was first a lawyer and later became a professor of theology in Oberlin, Ohio. William Ellery Channing was educated at Newport and at Harvard. In contrast, Joseph Smith received very little formal education. Yet, he did not claim to know about the Atonement from secular sources. He averred that the Lord Himself revealed these doctrines to him.

Joseph Smith was a literal prophet of God. There were over 1,000 years where a prophet did not guide mankind. Many preached of the Savior Jesus Christ and of the scriptures. However, with the restoration of a prophet, and in the first two years of the organized Church, Joseph Smith revealed a flood of knowledge that had not been generally taught in over 1,000 years. The Lord revealed through Joseph Smith at least eighty facets of His great sacrifice. Some of these insights confirmed what was taught elsewhere in scripture. Many of them clarified ideas that are incomplete or misinterpreted in scripture. However, a great many of these truths were not already found in scripture, but came solely through revelation. In review, these eighty points were as follows:

A Summary of Joseph Smith's Revelations about the Atonement

1. Jesus Christ related a firsthand account of the Atonement from the Savior, which appears to be recounted to inspire Martin Harris to sacrifice his money to publish the Book of Mormon (in short, Jesus Christ's great sacrifice was a reality and should be remembered to inspire mankind to make necessary sacrifices).

2. Jesus Christ literally sweat blood in Atonement for mankind.

3. Jesus Christ suffered both physically and spiritually in Gethsemane.

4. The Atonement was an act of submission to the will of the Father.

5. The atoning Savior subdued all things, including the power of the devil, to Himself.

6. Jesus Christ has the power to judge because of the Atonement.

7. The Atonement allows mankind to choose whether to repent or suffer.

8. The Lord revealed a foundational declaration regarding man's fallen condition and the Atonement.

9. The Lord instructed the Church to meet together often to partake of the sacrament to commemorate the Atonement, and indicated specific responsibilities of priests, teachers, and deacons regarding the sacrament. Those who wished to be baptized must first be instructed sufficiently about the gospel of Jesus Christ before partaking of the sacrament.

10. Moses testified that Jesus Christ is literally the Only Begotten Son of the Father in the flesh, an attribute necessary to complete the Atonement.

11. The Atonement of Jesus Christ transcends time, saving both those who lived before it occurred and those who would live afterwards.

12. Substitutions for bread and wine may be made in the sacrament, when necessity dictates.

13. Remembering the Atonement is more important than the symbols used in the sacrament.

14. Satan rebelled against the Atonement premortally, wanting to be the Savior himself, which caused him to be cast out of God's presence.

15. The Fall included spiritual death.

16. Animal sacrifice was a type and shadow of the Atonement.

17. Adam and Eve were forgiven for the Fall.

18. From Adam on, messengers taught mankind to utilize the Atonement through repentance.

19. All mankind will resurrect before the end of the world.

20. Through revelation, the Savior stated that He so loved the world that He gave his own life.

21. Revelation included a further witness that through the Atonement, mankind can become Jesus Christ's children, and become one with Him.

22. Denying the Atonement brings God's wrath.

23. The Savior would be born and atone for all mankind in the meridian of time.

24. Enoch preached a very instructive sermon on the Fall and its effects.

25. Adam utilized the Atonement through baptism.

26. Children are redeemed from the Fall by the Atonement.

27. Enoch used symbols of water, spirit, and blood to teach about the Atonement.

28. The Atonement empowered Jesus Christ to be mankind's advocate.

29. The Lord revealed to Enoch that the Savior would come after the Flood, and he saw Jesus Christ's coming and Atonement.

30. The Lord revealed to Enoch that the Savior would come through his lineage.

31. The Lord revealed to Enoch that Jesus Christ would be crucified.

32. The earth testified of the Atonement.

33. The Lord revealed to Enoch the effects of the Atonement on the dead.

34. There will be a resurrection of the just and a resurrection of the unjust, and those who died without the law and the gospel will resurrect with the just, if they accept the gospel in the hereafter.

35. Long before the Flood, Noah relentlessly urged his people to utilize the Atonement by repenting.

36. Old Testament prophets observed the sacrament.

37. Through the Atonement, Melchizedek and his people were translated.

38. The Lord taught Abraham about the Resurrection, and Abraham saw Jesus Christ's ministry.

39. People in Abraham's time wrongly distorted doctrines and practices regarding the Atonement by baptizing by sprinkling, baptizing children, and claiming Abel's blood was shed for a remission of sins.

40. Children are saved and covered by the Atonement until eight years old.

41. Those living at the Second Coming will be resurrected at their appointed time.

42. Existence between death and resurrection is a type of bondage.

43. The righteous will resurrect before the destruction of the wicked.

44. The Jews will grieve because of their iniquities and finally accept Jesus Christ as their Savior.

45. Multiple prophets, not just Isaiah, prophesied of Jesus Christ's miraculous birth.

46. Herod and his wise men declared that multiple prophets, in addition to Micah, prophesied that Jesus Christ would be born in Bethlehem.

47. Jesus Christ knew many years before his ministry began that He would complete the Atonement for all mankind.

48. John the Baptist testified of the Savior more boldly than is recorded in the KJV.

49. All true prophets testified of Jesus Christ.

50. Revelation clarified that Jesus Christ taught that forgiveness is always dependent on repentance.

51. The JST defined the teaching "take up your cross" as to deny ungodliness, worldly lusts, and to keep the commandments even when one doesn't particularly want to.

52. In the JST, the Savior taught specifically of the Atonement in conjunction with the sacrament, commanded the Apostles to continue to practice the ordinance, and the Apostles wept over their Savior during this emotional experience.

53. The Lord forgets mankind's sins when they confess and forsake them.

54. Jesus Christ can succor those who are tempted.

55. All living things will resurrect.

56. Jeremiah prophesied more about the Atonement and the facts surrounding it than are recorded in the KJV, particularly regarding what the chief priests would do with the money they used to bribe Judas to betray the Savior.

57. Pilate received stronger testimony that Jesus was innocent and truly the King of the Jews than is recorded in the KJV.

58. The JST corrected details regarding the Crucifixion and Resurrection, such as: the fact that Golgotha was a place of burial, that one of the two thieves hanging with Jesus defended the Savior's righteousness and asked the Lord to save him, that the Lord promised to teach that same thief in the world of the spirits, and that Mary Magda-

lene and other women found two angels testifying that the Savior had resurrected the Sunday morning after His Crucifixion.

59. Joseph Smith recorded that all the Saints from Adam to Jesus Christ's time resurrected soon after the Savior.

60. Elijah and Moses spoke to the Savior about his Atonement on the Mount of Transfiguration.

61. Jesus taught that God is not the God of the dead but of the living, because God will raise all the dead to life.

62. The JST revealed insights into Judas' betrayal, such as his offense at Jesus Christ's teaching, the Savior's warning to Judas not to betray innocent blood, and the possibility that the chief priests thought that Judas was sinning, as well as reconciling the two accounts of Judas' death.

63. For at least one moment, the Apostles doubted if Jesus Christ was the Messiah, even as He was in the process of saving them, and Jesus Christ knew their hearts.

64. The JST revealed at least a partial reason why the Apostles abandoned the Savior in the garden.

65. When given the decision between Jesus Christ and Barabbas, the crowd first cried out for Jesus to be delivered, then were persuaded to ask for Barabbas' release.

66. Revelation clarified Simeon's prophecy of Jesus Christ's death.

67. John the Baptist either used Isaiah's prophecy as a resource in his own prophetic teaching on the Atonement, or he quoted an unrecorded prophecy by Isaiah on the subject.

68. Jesus Christ asked the Father to forgive his Roman crucifiers while He was on the cross, not the unrepentant Jewish leaders who put him to death.

69. Revelation clarified John's testimony in John 1 that he believed Jesus Christ was chosen premortally and His gospel was preached before He made the earth, and that Jesus Christ was literally the Son of God.

70. Pondering the subject of the resurrection brought about a great vision on the resurrection and its effects on the

entire human race.

71. Joseph Smith saw the premortal and resurrected Savior in vision.

72. Jesus Christ, the only Savior for the entire universe, atoned for all the souls on worlds without number.

73. The Atonement will not cleanse sons of perdition.

74. The Atonement will sanctify the earth.

75. The great majority of the Father's children will inherit a kingdom of glory.

76. Revelation described the celestial kingdom and the characteristics of those that will inherit it.

77. Those who will inherit the celestial kingdom will gain celestial bodies.

78. Jesus Christ was spiritually the Firstborn of the Father.

79. Revelation described the terrestrial kingdom and the characteristics of those that will inherit it.

80. Revelation described the telestial kingdom and the characteristics of those that will inherit it.

The process by which Joseph Smith received these eighty insights illustrates some patterns in revelation. In some cases, the Lord revealed to the Prophet much at one time. For example, Doctrine and Covenants nineteen contains many priceless truths on the Atonement all in one place, revealed at the same time. And that time was even before the Church was organized. It was not gradual, but quick and powerful.

In contrast, it appears as though some revelations came, as Isaiah wrote, "precept upon precept; line upon line . . . here a little, and there a little" (Isaiah 28:10). In fact, in one instance Joseph Smith even quoted this Isaiah passage to describe the revelation process. [195] It is interesting to note that many times Joseph Smith's assignment to translate the Bible led to further revelation on a subject, and vice versa.

An example of this gradual revelation is the doctrine of the Atonement's effect on children. The Book of Mormon teaches that children were safe in the Atonement. The Lord revealed through Joseph Smith that children were not held accountable, and did not need to partake of the sacrament. Later, the Prophet recorded that Satan could not tempt children. Later still, the JST revealed that they were innocent until the age of eight. And finally, Doctrine and Covenants sixty-eight repeated this concept.

As another example, the JST indicated that the earth felt the unrighteousness of the people and cried to be sanctified. Revelation later taught that it would be sanctified and through the Atonement, the earth will become a celestial kingdom.

Perhaps the greatest example is the topic of resurrection. The Bible teaches that Jesus Christ resurrected, and that there will be a resurrection of the just and the unjust. The Book of Mormon, and later the Doctrine and Covenants, taught that the righteous, and those who did not receive divine law would take part in the first resurrection. The Lord revealed that the time between death and resurrection is bondage. Then, He taught that because of His Atonement, all things would resurrect. The JST intimates that all the Saints that had died before Jesus Christ, resurrected immediately after Him. Each doctrine built upon the previous until the Lord revealed—sparked by a verse Joseph Smith read in his work with the Bible—that resurrection would then lead to the celestial, terrestrial, or telestial kingdoms.

The Character of Jesus Christ and Those Involved in Events Surrounding the Atonement

In the JST and in revelations, the significance of Jesus Christ's existence is amplified even beyond most Bible verses. Before the earth was created, He was submissive to the Father and committed to be the Savior. He forgave Adam and Eve for the Fall. He sent Noah to plead for his people to repent before the Flood. He pled for those who died in the Flood. After He was born a mortal, at twelve, He taught the priests of the temple and knew of His impending sacrifice. No man could teach Him years before His public ministry. In fact, during His ministry He stated that He knew all things. He also taught and showed His submissiveness to and dependence on the Father. He was declared more often and more powerfully to be the word of God, and the way of salvation. And He, the greatest of all, trembled because of pain and bled from every pore in Atonement for all mankind.

Joseph Smith also recorded insights into supporting figures in events surrounding the Atonement. The JST and other revelations portray the Apostles to be more human, displaying mortal weaknesses.

They contended more often with one another. Their testimonies were more fragile. At least momentarily, they doubted that Jesus Christ was the Savior while He was suffering in Atonement. Judas was offended at Jesus Christ's teachings, and the Savior told him to beware of innocent blood before he betrayed the Redeemer. The chief priests were harsher and more condemning. Pilate received stronger testimony that Jesus was innocent. In short, in revelation, there was a greater divide between the character of Jesus Christ and the rest of mankind. Additional revelation portrayed the Savior as greater and more divine.

Joseph Smith Revealed the Greater Depth and Reach of the Atonement

The Lord revealed through Joseph Smith insights into the Atonement that simply enlighten the human mind. Jesus Christ's great sacrifice covered all of the souls that were born and died before the Savior was born into mortality. It worked retroactively. Jesus Christ also paid for all the sins, sicknesses, mortal weaknesses and death for all that came and will come after Him. Every child under the age of eight is saved through the Atonement. Every soul that ever lived on the earth will resurrect because of Jesus Christ. All living things, including the earth, plants, and animals will resurrect because of Jesus Christ. Every soul, with the exception of those in perdition, will inherit a kingdom of glory because of Jesus Christ. The same is true for every soul that lived, lives, or will live on one of countless worlds that the Savior created. In short, revelation through Joseph Smith testifies that every child of God has been and will be eternally affected by the life and Atonement of Jesus Christ.

The Atonement Was Planned and Taught from the Beginning

Revelation through Joseph Smith taught the plan of God. Jesus Christ agreed to be the Savior before the earth was created. The Atonement was not planned after the Fall, or as only a solution to the Fall, but both were part of a perfect plan of salvation. The Lord revealed this plan to Adam and Eve, and it was taught through the generations of the ancients. Enoch, Noah, and Abraham all knew of the future Atonement and taught about it. All prophets from the beginning taught about the Atonement. The ancient Church practiced the same saving ordinances, such as baptism, as the New Testament Church, and the Church today. They successfully utilized the Atonement to receive forgiveness and even eternal life.

Elder Dallin H. Oaks of the Quorum of the Twelve Apostles declared in General Conference, "Every follower of Jesus Christ knows that the most powerful ideas of the Christian faith are the resurrection and the atonement of Jesus Christ. Because of him we can be forgiven of our sins and we will live again." [196] The doctrines revealed through Joseph Smith were unique in many ways. He left a legacy of faith regarding these most powerful ideas. Today, millions believe in him and his teachings.

John Taylor, later a prophet of the Church wrote that "Joseph Smith, the Prophet and Seer of the Lord, has done more, save Jesus only, for the salvation of men in this world, than any other man that ever lived in it" (D&C 135:3). Joseph Smith deserved such verbal applause in many ways. Surely one of the ways that the Prophet did so much for the salvation of humanity was by revealing more truth about the Savior and how one can utilize His precious Atonement. Elder Oaks taught that the Resurrection and Atonement of Jesus Christ are "well known, but not well applied in the lives of most of us." [197] The Lord, through Joseph Smith, urged all to believe, repent, be baptized, and partake of the sacrament. He pleaded anciently for mankind and He still pleads for us. The Lord revealed through His Prophet hope for all mankind since the beginning, hope for every young child, hope for murderers and adulterers, hope for unknown souls on other worlds, hope for the righteous to receive all that the Father has, hope in Jesus Christ—truly the Savior of all mankind.

Endnotes

1. Joseph Smith, *Teachings of the Prophet Joseph Smith*, comp. Joseph Fielding Smith (Salt Lake City: Deseret Book, 1976), 366.

2. Joseph Smith, *History of The Church of Jesus Christ of Latter-day Saints*, ed. B. H. Roberts, 2d ed. rev., 7 vols. (Salt Lake City: The Church of Jesus Christ of Latter-day Saints, 1932–1951), 3:30.

3. Richard C. Edgely, "A Still, Small Voice and a Throbbing Heart," *Ensign*, May 2005, 11.

4. Bruce C. Hafen, "The Restored Doctrine of the Atonement," *Ensign*, December 1993, 7.

5. By mid-1832, the Prophet had made his corrections from Genesis 1 to Genesis 24:41 and throughout the entire New Testament. Though this is less than a third of the entire Bible, it was the text that saw the great majority of the changes.

6. After the First Vision, Joseph Smith received the first recorded revelation in July of 1828. The Prophet recorded that through the Book of Mormon, which was still being translated, that the Lamanites "may believe the gospel

and rely upon the merits of Jesus Christ, and be glorified
through faith in his name, and that through their repentance they might be saved" (D&C 3:20). In 1829, further
revelation stated the Lord's words, "I came unto my own,
and my own received me not. I am the light which shi-
neth in darkness, and the darkness comprehendeth it not"
(D&C 10:57–58). Revelations repeated this statement
three times over the next two months, and twice more
over the next two years (see D&C 6:21; D&C 10:57,
D&C 11:29; D&C 39:1–3; D&C 45:7–8). This was an
extremely brief synopsis of Jesus Christ's time in mortality and His Atonement. He came to His own people and
they did not receive Him in many ways, but surely the
Crucifixion is the most poignant example.

7. Dennis L. Largey, ed., *Book of Mormon Reference Compan-
    ion* (Salt Lake City: Deseret Book Company, 2003), 13.

8. Ibid., 14–15.

9. Ibid., 15.

10. This doctrine contrasts with Jonathan Edward's Calvinist
    view of limited Atonement. Edwards taught, "The suf-
    ferings of Christ answer the demands of the law, with
    respect to the sins of those who believe in him; and jus-
    tice is truly satisfied thereby." Jonathan Edwards, *Wisdom
    Displayed in Salvation*, WD VII, 92, as quoted in Conrad
    Cherry, *The Theology of Jonathan Edwards: A Reappraisal*
    (New York: Anchor Books, 1966), 93.

11. Joseph Fielding Smith taught, "It is an erroneous thought
    to believe that the Prophet selected all of the revelations
    he had received and placed them in the collection which
    was to become The Book of Commandments. Each of
    the revelations selected for that volume was placed there
    because the Prophet considered that it had some value
    to the Church in regard to its teachings. There are some
    revelations still in possession of the Church which were
    not included. Some of these we can readily believe were
    not included because the inspiration of the Prophet was
    that it was not necessary, or because some of them had an
    application which was not intended for publication and to

be sent to an unbelieving world." Joseph Fielding Smith, *Church History and Modern Revelation*, 4 vols. (Salt Lake City: The Church of Jesus Christ of Latter-day Saints, 1946–49) 1:248–249.

12. Joseph Smith, *History of The Church of Jesus Christ of Latter-day Saints*, ed. B. H. Roberts, 2d ed. rev., 7 vols. (Salt Lake City: The Church of Jesus Christ of Latter-day Saints, 1932–1951), 1:222 n. This number would be reduced to three thousand copies in 1832.

13. Joseph Fielding Smith, *Doctrines of Salvation*, 3 vols., ed. Bruce R. McConkie (Salt Lake City: Bookcraft, 1954–1956), 3:193.

14. The revelations found in the Book of Commandments are included in the Doctrine and Covenants. However, some early revelations that were omitted from the Book of Commandments were included in the Doctrine and Covenants. Such sections include D&C 2, 13, 17, 32, 51, and 57. It is interesting to note that sections 2 and 13, which were words from Moroni and John the Baptist, were omitted from the Book of Commandments. The original compilation of revelation consisted only of the Lord's own words (in one case spoken by an angel, which is now D&C 27).

15. *Joseph Smith's New Translation of the Bible: Original Documents*, ed. Scott H. Faulring, Kent P. Jackson, and Robert J. Matthews (Provo, Utah: Brigham Young University, 2004), 56; hereafter cited as *Joseph Smith's New Translation of the Bible*.

16. Smith, *History of the Church*, 1:238.

17. Robert J. Matthews, *Plainer Translation: Joseph Smith's Translation of the Bible* (Provo, Utah: Brigham Young University Press, 1975), 31; hereafter cited as *Plainer Translation*.

18. Smith, *History of the Church*, 1:324.

19. Ibid., 1:245.

20. Joseph Smith, *Teachings of the Prophet Joseph Smith*, 327.

21. Ibid., 310.

22. Joseph Smith to Frederick G. Williams, January 5, 1834, Joseph Smith Collection, Letters 1834, Church Historian's Office, Salt Lake City, Utah; quoted in Robert Millet, "From Translations to Revelations; Joseph Smith's Translation of the Bible and the Doctrine and Covenants," *Regional Studies in LDS History*, New York (BYU: 1992), 215–234; emphasis added.

23. *The New Testament with the Joseph Smith Translation*, comp. Stephen J. Hite and Julie M. Hite (Orem, Utah: The Veritas Group, 2001). And *The Old Testament with the Joseph Smith Translation*, comp. Stephen J. Hite and Julie M. Hite (Orem, Utah: The Veritas Group, 2001).

24. *Joseph Smith's New Translation of the Bible*, 56.

25. Elder B. H. Roberts wrote the following about D&C 19: "There are few revelations that have been given in the present dispensation of the Gospel more important than this one . . . [it is] of first importance in the doctrinal development of the Church" (Joseph Smith, *HC*, 1:72 footnote). It is interesting to note that such a doctrinally significant revelation preceded the organization of the Church.

26. D&C 19:18 added the phrase "and to suffer" before "both body and spirit" to the Book of Commandments (see Book of Commandments 16:18).

27. Joseph Smith, *Lectures on Faith* (Salt Lake City: Deseret Book, 1995) 6:7.

28. Isaiah wrote that the Savior will come in reminding red robes at His Second Coming (see Isaiah 63:1; D&C 133:46).

29. Lucy Mack Smith, *History of Joseph Smith By His Mother* (Salt Lake City: Deseret Book Company, 1996), 165.

30. Ibid., 166, 171.

31. Jesus Christ referred to Himself as "him who has all power" in later revelation (D&C 61:1). Paul also testified that the Savior was "able even to subdue all things unto himself" (Philippians 3:21).

32. Noah Webster, *American Dictionary of the English Language: Noah Webster 1828* (San Francisco: The Foundation for American Christian Education, 1993).

33. Several General Authorities of the Church have explained why Jesus Christ has such power over Satan. One such reason is that He faced Satan and withstood him during the Atonement. Elder Boyd K. Packer taught that Jesus Christ "faced the awesome power of the evil one who was not confined to flesh nor subject to mortal pain. That was Gethsemane!" in "Atonement, Agency, Accountability," *Ensign*, May 1988, 69. Elder James E. Talmage also taught, "In that hour of anguish Christ met and overcame all the horrors that Satan, 'the prince of this world' could inflict" in *Jesus the Christ* (Salt Lake City: The Church of Jesus Christ of Latter-day Saints, 1981), 613. Jesus Christ faced and conquered the devil during the Atonement.

34. John Wesley, *Wesley's Notes on the Bible* (Grand Rapids: The Zondervan Corporation, 1987), 451.

35. The word "devils" is found in the Old Testament (see Leviticus 17:7; Deuteronomy 32:17; 2 Chronicles 11:15; Psalm 106:37).

36. This insight is found in W. Jeffery Marsh, *The Joseph Smith Translation: Precious Truths Restored* (American Fork: Covenant Communications, Inc., 2002), 77.

37. Later revelation promised Joseph Smith and Sidney Rigdon that if they kept His commandments and covenants that "Satan shall tremble" (D&C 35:24).

38. This doctrine was also taught in the Book of Mormon (see Alma 11:44; Mormon 3:20, 7:6; Ether 12:38; Moroni 8:21).

39. Joseph Smith later revealed Enoch's sermon on the Fall and Atonement in which He termed the Savior as "righteous Judge" (Moses 6:57).

40. In Luke, the Savior taught with similar boldness, "Except ye shall repent, ye shall . . . perish" (Luke 13:3), but this does not mention Christ-like suffering.

41. Joseph Smith, *HC*, 1:79.

42. These revelations, or series of revelations, are hard to definitively place chronologically. Joseph Smith recorded that the Lord revealed it "from time to time" (Joseph Smith, *HC*, 1:64). Portions of this revelation were probably given as early as late 1829, but the majority was received and declared in April of 1830 with the organization of the Church (Robert J. Woodford, "The Historical Development of the Doctrine and Covenants," 2 vols. Ph.D. dissertation, [Provo: Brigham Young University, 1974], 1:290).

43. Joseph Smith, *HC*, 1:61.

44. The Doctrine and Covenants now reads that Apostles should "administer bread and wine—the emblems of the flesh and blood of Christ—" (D&C 20:40).

45. The Bible does recount what the Savior said to His Apostles during the sacrament. Matthew wrote, "Jesus took bread, and blessed it, and brake it, and give it to the disciples, and said, Take, eat; this is my body. And he took the cup, and gave thanks, and gave it to them, saying, Drink ye all of it" (Matthew 26:26–27). Paul recorded, "When he had given thanks, he brake it, and said, Take, eat: this is my body, which is broken for you: this do in remembrance of me" (1 Cor. 11:24). However, the Bible does not include a record of what Jesus Christ said to His Father to bless or give thanks for the sacrament.

46. Joseph Smith, *HC*, 1:85.

47. Joseph Smith, *HC*, 1:91. Joseph Smith recorded in July of 1830, "I have lifted thee up out of thine afflictions, and have counseled thee, that thou has been delivered from all thine enemies, and thou hast been delivered from the powers of Satan and from darkness" (D&C 24:1). Again, Jesus Christ noted that He had power over Satan.

48. During June of 1830, Joseph Smith wrote, "I will say . . . that amid all the trials and tribulations we had to wade through, the Lord, who well knew our infantile and delicate situation, vouchsafed for us a supply of strength, and

granted us 'line upon line of knowledge—here a little and there a little,' of which the following was a precious morsel" (Joseph Smith, *HC*, 1:98). Joseph Smith then recorded the "visions of Moses." These visions would be the first chapter in the JST, and later the first chapter of Moses in the Pearl of Great Price. Joseph Smith did not specify whether he received this revelation as part of the translation process or not, however, the text is included in each of the three Old Testament JST manuscripts. The visions of Moses are introduced with the title "A Revelation given to Joseph the Revelator June 1830" in both of our earliest manuscripts of the JST. This information is found in Robert J. Matthews, *A Plainer Translation: Joseph Smith's New Translation of the Bible* (Provo: Brigham Young University Press, 1975), 62, 64, hereafter cited as *Plainer Translation*. The exact date when the Prophet began his new translation is unknown. Joseph Smith and Oliver Cowdery bought a King James Version of the Bible from E. B. Grandin on October 8, 1829. Whether or not they did so planning to begin the new translation is left to conjecture (Matthews, *Plainer Translation*, 26). However, the manuscripts of the JST verify that Joseph Smith received Moses 1 in June of 1830. Matthews, *Plainer Translation*, 27.

49. Joseph Smith, *Teachings*, 323.

50. The reference to the "Only Begotten" in Moses 1:21 was not in the original manuscripts, but was adapted into the Pearl of Great Price based on the 1867 RLDS edition of the JST. This information is found in Robert Matthews, *A Bible! A Bible!* (Salt Lake City; Bookcraft, 1990), 109.

51. Joseph Smith also added the title to 1 Timothy 2:4. It had already been stated in the Book of Mormon nine times (see 2 Nephi 25:12; Jacob 4:5, 11; Alma 5:48; 9:26; 12:33, 34; 13:5, 9).

52. This passage reads a little differently in the Doctrine and Covenants. It states that the Atonement will save "not only those who believed after he came in the meridian of time, in the flesh, but all those from the beginning,

even as many as were before he came, who believed in the words of the holy prophets . . . as well as those who should come after" (D&C 20:26–27).

53. In this vision, God instructed Moses to worship and pray in the name of the Savior (Moses 1:17–18). Perhaps this is symbolic that the only way to reach the Father is through His Son.

54. Joseph Smith, *HC*, 1:104.

55. Joseph Smith, *HC*, 1:106.

56. The Lord also later instructed the Saints to partake of the sacrament as part of Sabbath day observance (see D&C 59:9–11).

57. Joseph Smith, *Joseph Smith's New Translation of the Bible*, 56.

58. In February of 1832, Joseph Smith had a vision, which included the premortal drama. In the account of this vision, the Prophet described Jesus Christ as He "whom the Father loved and who was in the bosom of the Father" (D&C 76:25). This wording confirms the feeling and doctrine of Moses 4:2.

59. Orson Pratt in *Journal of Discourses*, (London: Latter-day Saints Book Depot, 1854–1886) 15:249.

60. Joseph Smith also referred to Satan as an angel in JST Revelation 9:1.

61. Joseph Smith later wrote about Satan in the premortal life, "And I saw and bear record of warfare in heav'n; / For an angel of light, in authority great, / Rebell'd against Jesus, and sought for his pow'r, / But was thrust down to woe from his Glorified state." *Times and Seasons*, Feb. 1, 1843.

62. First-fruit offerings are not introduced until the Law of Moses (see Leviticus 6:14–18).

63. Joseph Smith, *Teachings*, 58. John Wesley taught similarly, "Cain's [offering] was only a sacrifice of acknowledge-ment offered to the Creator; but Abel brought a sacri-fice of atonement, the blood which was shed in order to

remission, thereby owning himself a sinner, deprecating God's wrath, and imploring his favor in a Mediator. But the great difference was, Abel offered in faith and Cain did not. Abel offered with an eye to God's will as his rule and in dependence upon the promise of a Redeemer. But Cain did not offer in faith, and so it turned into sin to him." (John Wesley, *Wesley's Notes on the Bible*, 29.)

64. George Whitefield was educated at Pembroke College, Oxford, where he was influenced by John Wesley, and his brother Charles Wesley. He became famous for his revival meetings, which he took through the British Isles and the American Colonies. He made seven preaching tours of the Colonies between 1738 and 1770. The three preachers mentioned above, passed away years before the birth of Joseph Smith, but their ideas were influential in the Prophet's day.

65. George Whitefield, *Memoirs*, 316–317.

66. George Whitefield, *Memoirs*, 322.

67. George Whitefield, *Memoirs*, 313.

68. Alexander Campbell was an American preacher who founded the Disciples of Christ, also known as the Camp-bellites. He based his beliefs on the New Testament and taught against emotional revivalism.

69. Alexander Campbell, *Popular Lectures and Addresses* (St. Louis: John Burns, 1861), 213–214.

70. John Wesley was educated at Christ Church, Oxford University. He is credited with founding and uniting many Methodist congregations. He was a famous preacher to the layman in England and organized and ordained preachers to serve in the American Colonies.

71. John Wesley, *Wesley's Notes on the Bible*, 27.

72. John Wesley, *A Compend of Wesley's Theology*, eds. Robert W. Burtner and Robert E. Chiles (Nashville: Abingdon Press, n.d.), 65.

73. George Whitefield, *Memoirs*, 312.

74. George Whitefield, *Memoirs*, 312.

75. Alexander Campbell taught that Adam "certainly was the oracle of the world for the first thousand years of its history" (Alexander Campbell, *Popular Lectures and Addresses*, 110). Adam guided his posterity to the Savior through repentance.

76. Joseph Smith, *Teachings*, 271.

77. He also testified of His Resurrection in D&C 6:37; 18:11–12.

78. Joseph Smith, *HC*, 1:127–128.

79. *Times and Seasons*, Feb. 1, 1843.

80. In March of 1831, Joseph Smith recorded what is now D&C 45. This revelation contained the Lord's voice testifying that those who received Him, "gave I power . . . to become the sons of God" as well as "power to obtain eternal life" (D&C 45:8). In January of 1831 a revelation repeated this truth to James Covill (see D&C 39:4). The revelation of March 1831 repeated this truth again, and added the phrase, "And even unto them that believed on my name gave I power to obtain eternal life" (D&C 45:8). Jesus Christ has and will give to men and women power to gain eternal life. Paul also taught this concept in Romans 8:15–17.

81. Joseph Smith had already recorded this phrase in a revelation in April of 1830 (see D&C 20:26). It is also used in D&C 39:3; Moses 6:57, 62; 7:46.

82. The Book of Mormon is different. Nephi knew that the Savior would be born in 600 years (see 1 Nephi 19:8). Later in the Book of Mormon, Samuel the Lamanite prophesied that Jesus Christ would be born in 5 years (see Helaman 14:2).

83. Joseph Fielding Smith wrote a definition of the "meridian of time": "Moreover, our Savior came in the meridian of time. That dispensation is called the dispensation of the meridian of time. This means that it was about half way from the beginning of 'time' to the end of 'time.' Anyone

who desires can figure it for himself that our Lord came about 4,000 years from the time of the fall. The millennium is to come some time following the 2,000 years after his coming. Then there is to be the millennium for 1,000 years, and following that a 'little season,' the length of which is not revealed, but which may bring 'time' to its end about 8,000 years from the beginning." Joseph Fielding Smith, *Doctrines of Salvation*, 1:81.

84. Joseph Smith, *HC*, 131–133.

85. According to Joseph Smith, Enoch visited both Jude and Paul, the author of Hebrews (see Joseph Smith, *Teachings*, 170).

86. Jonathan Edwards, *Images or Shadows of Divine Things*, ed. Perry Miller (New Haven: Yale University Press, 1948), 91, as quoted in Conrad Cherry, *The Theology of Jonathan Edwards: A Reappraisal* (New York: Anchor Books, 1966), 59.

87. George Whitefield, *Memoirs*, 371, 418, 457.

88. George Whitefield, *Memoirs*, 458–459.

89. John Wesley, *Wesley's Notes on the Bible*, 31.

90. G. Frederick Wright, *Charles Grandison Finney* (Cambridge: The Riverside Press, 1891), 230.

91. William Ellery Channing, *Selected Writings*, 94.

92. It is interesting to note that though baptism was not mentioned in the Old Testament, according to the JST John the Baptist was not the only one baptizing in the New Testament. Sometime between April and June of 1831, Joseph Smith made a significant addition to Matthew 9:16 (*Joseph Smith's New Translation of the Bible*, 57). "Then said the Pharisees unto him [Jesus Christ], Why will ye not receive us with our baptism, seeing we keep the whole law?" (JST Matthew 9:16). The Pharisees, the sect known for its strict obedience to the law, were baptizing. It was part of the law. This was not a new addition, but practiced since the law was given. In the JST, the Savior responded to the Pharisees, "I receive not you with

your baptism, because it profiteth nothing" (JST Matthew 9:16).

93. Joseph Smith, *HC*, 2:16–17.

94. George Whitefield, *Memoirs*, 323.

95. Interestingly, as early as June 1829, Joseph Smith recorded that children "who have arrived at the years of accountability" need to repent of their sins (D&C 18:42).

96. This does not mean that Enoch and his people were resurrected at that time. The Prophet Joseph Smith said, "Many have supposed that the doctrine of translation was a doctrine whereby men were taken immediately into the presence of God, and into an eternal fullness, but this is a mistaken idea. Their place of habitation is that of the terrestrial order, and a place prepared for such characters He held in reserve to be ministering angels unto many planets, and who as yet have not entered into so great a fullness as those who are resurrected from the dead" (Joseph Smith, *Teachings*, 170).

97. The dictionary continues to define advocate as "one who pleads the cause of another" in both civil court and tribunals, or "one who defends, vindicates, or espouses a cause, by argument; one who is friendly to; as, an *advocate* for peace, or for the oppressed" (Noah Webster, *American Dictionary of the English Language: Noah Webster 1828* [San Francisco: The Foundation for American Christian Education, 1993]).

98. The JST adds to the previously mentioned verse, 1 John 2:1, that "if any man sin, *and repent*, we have an advocate with the Father" (JST 1 John 2:1, italics added). This emphasizes the importance of repenting to receive all of the benefits of Jesus Christ's advocacy. Also, D&C 62:1 makes another reference to the Savior's role as advocate.

99. The Bible, by itself, without the revelations given through Joseph Smith, testified of this truth after the fact (see Luke 3:37). There are also several verses indicating that the Savior would come out of David's seed (see Isaiah 9:7; Jeremiah 23:5; Psalm 132:11).

100. The Psalms prophesied that Jesus Christ's hands and feet would be pierced, and that none of His bones would be broken (see Psalms 22:16; 34:20). Isaiah prophesied that Jesus Christ would be fastened "as a nail in a sure place" (Isaiah 22:23). The Savior Himself used the example of Moses lifting up the brazen serpent to prophesy that He would also be lifted up (see John 3:14).

101. It is significant that both of these visions were revealed through Joseph Smith.

102. It is noteworthy that this vision of Jesus Christ's Crucifixion, as graphic as it may have been, caused Enoch to rejoice. He happily testified that Jesus Christ would complete the Atonement. And he testified referring to the event in the present tense, "The Righteous *is* lifted up . . . the Lamb *is* slain" (Moses 7:47, italics added). Perhaps Enoch used such language to indicate that the Atonement was as good as accomplished. The ancient prophet was so confident in the Atonement and its power that he declared, "and through faith I *am* in the bosom of the Father; and behold, Zion is with me!" (Moses 7:47, italics added).

103. The whole face of the earth will change in order for it to be renewed. On November 3, 1831, Joseph Smith recorded that the Lord will "break down the mountains, and the valleys shall not be found. He shall command the great deep, and it shall be driven back into the north countries, and the islands shall become one land; and the land of Jerusalem and the land of Zion shall be turned back into their own place, and the earth shall be like as it was in the days before it was divided" (D&C 133:22–24). The Lord will reverse the effects of the Fall.

104. Joseph Smith, *Teachings*, 181.

105. *Times and Seasons*, Feb. 1, 1843.

106. The prophet Ezra Taft Benson taught, "The Lord promised, therefore, that righteousness would come from heaven and truth out of the earth. We have seen the marvelous fulfillment of that prophecy in our generation. The

Book of Mormon has come forth out of the earth, filled
with truth, serving as the very 'keystone of our religion.'
God has also sent down righteousness from heaven. The
Father Himself appeared with His Son to the Prophet
Joseph Smith. The angel Moroni, John the Baptist, Peter,
James, and numerous other angels were directed by heaven
to restore the necessary powers to the kingdom. Further,
the Prophet Joseph Smith received revelation after revelation from the heavens during those first critical years of
the Church's growth. These revelations have been preserved for us in the Doctrine and Covenants." "The Gift
of Modern Revelation," *Ensign*, November 1986, 78.

107. Five years later, in November of 1835, Joseph Smith
quoted Moses 7:47 and gave the following insight, "Now
I understand by this quotation, that God clearly manifested to Enoch the redemption which He prepared, by
offering the Messiah as a Lamb slain from before the
foundation of the world; and by virtue of the same, the
glorious resurrection of the Savior, and the resurrection of
all the human family, even a resurrection of their corpo-
real bodies, is brought to pass; and also righteousness and
truth are to sweep the earth as with a flood. And now, I
ask, how righteousness and truth are going to sweep the
earth as with a flood? I will answer. Men and angels are
to be co-workers in bringing to pass this great work, and
Zion is to be prepared, even a new Jerusalem, for the elect
that are to be gathered from the four quarters of the earth,
and to be established an holy city, for the tabernacle of the
Lord shall be with them" *Messenger and Advocate*, (Kirtland), November 1835.

108. Joseph Smith, *HC*, 1:145.

109. *Joseph Smith's New Translation of the Bible*, 64, 78. Also,
Joseph Smith recorded that "soon after the words of
Enoch were given," the Lord commanded him to pause
in his translation until he had moved to Ohio (Joseph
Smith, *HC*, 1:39).

110. With the exclusion of John 5:29, all these verses remain
unaltered in the JST.

111. The concept of the "first resurrection" was also taught in Mosiah 18:9 and Alma 40:15–17.

112. John Wesley taught that though the men of Noah's day were so wicked, "it cannot indeed be denied but many of them perhaps all, had good motions put into their hearts. For the spirit of God did then also 'strive with man,' if haply he might repent, more especially during that gracious reprieve, the hundred and twenty years while the ark was preparing," John Wesley, *Wesley's Sermons: An Anthology*, ed. Albert C Outler and Richard P. Heitzenrater (Nashville: Abingdon Press, 1991), 328.

113. Interestingly, the Book of Mormon added information on the ancient high priest. Alma preached that Melchizedek's people were "full of all manner of wickedness," but the king and high priest "exercised mighty faith, . . . did preach repentance . . . And behold, they did repent" (Alma 13:17–18). Alma testified that "none were greater" than Melchizedek (Alma 13:19). Alma also mentioned that what he said was sufficient because apparently the people had scriptural account of Melchizedek's people (see Alma 13:20).

114. Bruce R. McConkie taught, "The sacrament of the Lord's supper is an ordinance of salvation in which all the faithful must participate if they are to live and reign with him. It may well have been prefigured, some two thousand years before its formal institution among men when 'Melchizedek, king of Salem, brought forth bread and wine; and he brake bread and blest it, and he blest the wine, he being the priest of the most high God. And he gave to Abram.' (JST Genesis 14:17–18)." Bruce R. McConkie, *The Promised Messiah* (Salt Lake City: Deseret Book Company, 1978), 384. Interestingly Jonathan Edwards taught, "The bread and wine [Melchizedek brought] signified the same blessings of the covenant of grace that the bread and wine does in the sacrament of the Lord's Supper. So that as Abraham had a seal of the covenant in circumcision that was equivalent to baptism, so now he had a seal of it equivalent to the Lord's Supper." Jonathan Edwards, *Works of Jonathan*

Edwards, vol. 9. ed. John F. Wilson (New Haven: Yale University Press, 1989), 163.

115. Joseph Smith, *HC*, 2: 16. Also, Wilford Woodruff taught, "The ordinances of the Gospel have never been changed from the days of Adam to the present time, and never will be to the end of time." Wilford Woodruff in *Journal of Discourses*, 24:239–240.

116. Blood was sprinkled in the act of sacrifice, which may have led to some confusion between the symbolism of baptism and sacrifice.

117. George Whitefield, *Memoirs*, 421.

118. John Wesley, *A Compend of Wesley's Theology*, 269.

119. Of course during the Millennium there will only be righteous people.

120. *Joseph Smith's New Translation of the Bible*, 57.

121. James Mulholland later wrote in Joseph Smith's journal that he "explained concerning the coming of the Son of Man &c that all will be raised to meet him, but the righteous will remain with him in the cloud whilst all the proud and all that do wickedly will have to return to the earth and suffer his vengeance which he will take upon them this is the second death &c &c." Joseph Smith, *The Words of Joseph Smith*, 15. See also D&C 88:95–104.

122. Joseph Smith made changes to these verses. The Prophet added phrases to again testify that the righteous dead will resurrect and be taken up into the cloud with the righteous who are living at the time of the Second Coming: "For this we say unto you by the word of the Lord, that *they who* are alive *at* the coming of the Lord shall not prevent them *who remain* [the dead] *unto the coming of the Lord who* are asleep. For the Lord himself shall descend from heaven with a shout, with the voice of the archangel, and with the trump of God; and the dead in Christ shall rise first; Then *they who* are alive, shall be caught up together *into* the clouds *with them who remain*, to meet the Lord in the air" (JST 1 Thessalonians 4:15–17; italics indicate JST changes).

123. Joseph Smith had previously translated prophetic teaching in the Book of Mormon about the Jews being converted to Jesus Christ and restored to His fold (see 1 Nephi 15:19; 2 Nephi 26:12; 30:2, 7; Jacob 4:15; Mormon 3:21; 5:14).

124. Joseph Smith added that Matthew acknowledged that the story of the Savior's birth was already written at his time (see JST Matthew 1:18).

125. The JST also added a simple clarifying line to one of Jeremiah's prophecies that Matthew quoted. This verse foretold of the merciless murdering of all infants under the age of two at the time of Jesus Christ. "In Rama*h* there *was* a voice heard, lamentation, and weeping, and great mourning, Rachel weeping *for the loss of* her children, and would not be comforted, because they *were* not" (JST Matthew 2:18; italics indicate changes in the JST).

126. Joseph Smith later taught on this same theme, "When still a boy He [Christ] had all the intelligence necessary to enable Him to rule and govern the kingdom of the Jews, and could reason with the wisest and most profound doctors of law and divinity, and make their theories and practice to appear like folly compared with the wisdom He possessed; but He was a boy only, and lacked physical strength even to defend His own person; and was subject to cold, to hunger and to death" (Joseph Smith, *Teachings*, 392). Also, On May 6, 1833, Joseph Smith recorded John the Baptist's testimony that is not included in the New Testament. In this testimony, John related some interesting concepts about Jesus Christ's youth. John testified that premortally the Lord was "full of grace and truth," but when born mortally "he received not of the fulness at first" (D&C 93:11–12). This revelation taught that the Redeemer was not born with the fullness of the Father. John the Baptist then testified that the young Savior grew, receiving "grace for grace; and he received not of the fullness at first, but continued from grace to grace, until he received a fulness" (D&C 93:12–13). These verses should give all humanity hope. Jesus Christ Himself went

through the same process man must go through to reach exaltation. He grew little by little, grace to grace until he "received a fulness of the glory of the Father" (D&C 93:16). In fact, the Lord shared John's testimony so that mankind could know how to successfully follow Jesus Christ's example of obedience and growth until they also gained a fullness (see D&C 93:19–20).

127. This occasion was extremely fitting in light of previously discussed JST changes. Sons were circumcised when eight days old to symbolize the baptism that would come. On the occasion when John was circumcised, Zacharias prophesied of his son's great work with baptisms.

128. Also during this time period, Joseph Smith adds that Jesus Christ testified that it was prophetically written, "Behold, I will send my messenger and he shall prepare the way before me" (JST Matt 17:11–12). This is a quotation of Malachi 3:1. Jesus Christ and Gospel authors quoted this verse several other times (see Matt 11:10; Mark 1:2; Luke 1:17; 7:27).

129. On May 6, 1833, Joseph Smith quoted a portion of John the Baptist's testimony of Jesus Christ that is not found in scripture: "I saw his glory, that he was in the beginning, before the world was; Therefore, in the beginning the Word was, for he was the Word, even the messenger of salvation—the light and the Redeemer of the world; the Spirit of truth, who came into the world, because the world was made by him, and in him was the life of men and the light of men. The worlds were made by him; men were made by him; all things were made by him, and through him, and of him. And I, John, bear record that I beheld his glory, as the glory of the Only Begotten of the Father, full of grace and truth, even the Spirit of truth, which came and dwelt in the flesh, and dwelt among us . . . And I, John, bear record, and lo, the heavens were opened, and the Holy Ghost descended upon him in the form of a dove, and sat upon him, and there came a voice out of heaven saying: This is my beloved Son. And I, John, bear record that he received a fulness of the glory of

the Father; and he received all power, both in heaven and on earth, and the glory of the Father was with him, for he dwelt in him" (D&C 93:7–11, 15–17). John the Baptist had a clear testimony of Jesus Christ's premortal life, His actions as Creator, His divine Sonship, and that the Savior received all power.

130. Another noteworthy verse warns that if there were ancient leaders who did not testify of Him, they were not prophets at all, but "thieves and robbers" (JST John 10:8).

131. Joseph Smith, *HC*, 1:170.

132. *Joseph Smith's New Translation of the Bible*, 57.

133. Bruce R. McConkie wrote, "the scribes were referring to some passage of scripture available to them, but since lost from the knowledge of men"—*Doctrinal New Testament Commentary*, 3 vols. (Salt Lake City: Bookcraft, 1976), 1:276).

134. Joseph Smith recorded later that mankind cannot be forgiven for shedding innocent blood (see D&C 132:27).

135. Joseph Smith, *Teachings*, 358.

136. Joseph Smith, *Teachings*, 358.

137. Joseph Smith had already translated the words of Jacob who taught a similar doctrine: "believe in Christ, and view his death, and suffer his cross and bear the shame of the world" (Jacob 1:8).

138. The Apostles would have been familiar with crucifixion as a mode of execution, but did they know that Jesus Christ would die the same way? The Psalmist gave clues about the Savior's death, and the Savior taught that He would be "lifted up" (John 3:14). Whether or not the Apostles pieced these teachings together to know that Jesus Christ would be crucified is unknown. This paper has already discussed Enoch's and Nephi's vision, even Nephi's reference to the writings of Neum and Zenock on the subject. However, it is unknown how many, if any, of these prophecies were available to and understood by the Apostles. It is certain, however, that the Savior's

words could have easily returned to the Apostles' minds as Jesus Christ took up his cross, as He sacrificed and obeyed. The JST also adds one reference to taking up one's cross to the Sermon on the Mount (JST Matt 5:28). In this instance, the Savior used the imagery of taking up one's cross to discourage adultery. This, however, was not new revelation, but brought the New Testament account into harmony with Jesus Christ's equivalent sermon in the Book of Mormon, which was previously revealed (3 Nephi 12:30).

139. Joseph Smith recorded a repetition of this phrase in July of 1837 (see D&C 112:14).

140. Matt 9:2–26:1 was translated sometime between April 7, and June 19, 1831 (*Joseph Smith's New Translation of the Bible*, 57). This obviously included Matthew 16. Joseph Smith recorded Doctrine and Covenants 53 in June of 1831. If there was any sort of regularity in the translation, Joseph Smith would have translated Matthew 16 in May.

141. Paul also used the word once in a letter to Timothy describing the Atonement (see 1 Timothy 2:6).

142. The JST adds that Jesus Christ said this very clearly, "Remember me in this hour that I was with you and drank with you of this cup, even the last time in my ministry" (JST Mark 14:24).

143. *Joseph Smith's New Translation of the Bible*, 57. As was previously mentioned, records indicate that Joseph Smith made changes from Matthew 9:2—26:71 from 7 April to before June 19, 1831. Because the sacrament story occurs in the last chapter of that section, if there was any regularity to the translation, changes were made closer to June 19, 1831.

144. Joseph Smith, *HC*, 1:199.

145. Joseph Smith made an addition to the thirtieth Psalm that is reminiscent of this truth. The JST reads, "For his [God's] anger kindleth against the wicked; they repent, and in a moment it is turned away, and they are in his favor, and he giveth them life" (JST Psalms 30:5).

146. Joseph Smith, *The Words of Joseph Smith*, 72.

147. Joseph Smith, *Teachings*, 291–292. This quotation continues on to say that this idea flies in the face of the interpretations of Joseph Smith's day, but that such interpretations are flat as a pancake.

148. Joseph Smith, *HC*, 1:215.

149. *Joseph Smith's New Translation of the Bible*, 57.

150. The only possible candidates in Jeremiah are 18:2–6; 19:1–13; and 32:6–15. In these verses Jeremiah did visit a potter and buy a field. However, these verses are not a clear allusion to Judas. In fact, any such connection with the current translation would take some creative reasoning. Interestingly, Joseph Smith made no additions to the book of Jeremiah that would indicate such a prophecy.

151. John Wesley, *Wesley's Notes on the Bible*, 423.

152. The JST of the same account in Mark is similar: "And Jesus answering said unto him, I am, even as thou sayest" (JST Mark 15:2).

153. Joseph Smith also changed the color of the robe placed on Jesus Christ by the Roman soldiers in Matthew 27:28 from red to purple (see JST Matthew 27:28). This put the color in harmony with Mark 15:17 and John 19:2.

154. Joseph Smith, *Teachings*, 309.

155. Alexander Campbell taught, "There is no intimation that human spirits dwell in human bodies after death, or that they are interred with them in their graves. To this agree the words of Matthew xxvi. 52,53:—After our Lord's resurrection, when the graves were opened, 'many bodies of the saints arose, went into Jerusalem and appeared unto many.' Now, had the spirits of theses saints been sleeping in their bodies, would it not have been said, many of the 'saints arose, went into Jerusalem and appeared unto many'? The fact that bodies only came out of these graves, will be regarded as proof that bodies only were deposited in them" (Alexander Campbell, *Popular Lectures and Addresses*, 442).

156. Joseph Smith, Discourse of May 16th, 1841, reported in *Times and Seasons (November 1840–October 1841)*, Vol. 2, No. 15, June 1, 1841, 430.

157. Joseph Smith, *HC*, 1:238.

158. *Joseph Smith's New Translation of the Bible*, 57.

159. Joseph Smith, *Teachings*, 67–68.

160. The JST added the declaration that Gethsemane was a garden (JST Mark 14:32).

161. Joseph Smith also added that it was the tired, doubting Apostles, not the Lord, who said, "the spirit truly is ready, but the flesh is weak" (JST Mark 14:38).

162. Joseph Smith, *The Papers of Joseph Smith*, 39.

163. With the JST changes to this verse it appears as though Barabbas had been released on such an occasion before (see JST Mark 15:11).

164. In the JST, the crowd shouted, "deliver him unto us to be crucified" (JST Mark 15:13).

165. Either the JST quotation refers to another prophecy of the Atonement, which is unusually similar, or these verses of the New Testament provide an inspired version of the Old. In either case, the Atonement is at the forefront of the prophecy.

166. Joseph Smith, *HC*, 1:241.

167. Joseph Smith, *HC*, 1:242.

168. There are several other changes related to the doctrine that Jesus Christ is the literal Son of God. Peter proclaimed that the Savior was "the Son of the living God" (Matthew 16:16). The JST added those very words to the same story in Mark, and added that Jesus Christ was the Son of God to the account in Luke (JST Mark 8:29; JST Luke 9:20). The JST also added the title "the Son" to the Savior in John 6:44 (JST John 6:44). Jesus Christ Himself boldly declared that God was His Father. Though in Mark 10:23 Jesus Christ spoke of the "kingdom of God," according to the JST, Jesus Christ spoke more personally

of the "kingdom of my Father" (JST Mark 10:23). There are four additional references in the JST that depict Jesus Christ as the Son of God (see JST Matthew 12:50; JST Luke 21:36; JST John 6:44; JST Revelation 1:7).

169. Joseph Smith, *HC*, 1:245.

170. Philo Dibble, *Juvenile Instructor*, 15 May 1892, 303–304, quoted in Stephen E. Robinson and H. Dean Garrett, *A Commentary on the Doctrine and Covenants*, vol. 2 (Salt Lake City: Deseret Book Company, 2001), 286–287.

171. Joseph Smith, *HC*, 1:252–253.

172. Joseph Smith, *HC*, 5:402.

173. Times and Seasons, 1 February 1, 1843.

174. In the poetic interpretation, the Prophet wrote, "And besides him there ne'er was a Savior of men" *Times and Seasons*, February 1, 1843.

175. *Times and Seasons*, February 1, 1843.

176. Joseph Smith wrote to W. W. Phelps in 1833, "Say to the brothers Hulet and to all others, that the Lord never authorized them to say that the devil, his angels, or the sons of perdition, should ever be restored; for their state of destiny was not revealed to man, is not revealed, nor ever shall be revealed, save to those who are made partakers thereof: consequently those who teach this doctrine have not received it of the Spirit of the Lord. Truly Brother Oliver declared it to be the doctrine of devils. We, therefore, command that this doctrine be taught no more in Zion. We sanction the decision of the Bishop and his council, in relation to this doctrine being a bar to communion." Joseph Smith, *Teachings*, 24.

177. Joseph Smith, *Teachings*, 358.

178. Joseph Smith, *Teachings*, 358.

179. Joseph Smith, *The Words of Joseph Smith*, 60. Joseph Smith first distinguished between these two terms in the JST of Matthew 24. See Joseph Smith—Matthew 1:4, 55 (*The Words of Joseph Smith*, 25, footnote 9). Interestingly this was first done in 1831.

180. *Times and Seasons*, February 1, 1843.

181. George Whitefield, *Memoirs*, 376, 435.

182. George Whitefield, *Memoirs*, 438.

183. Richard Baxter, *Works* vol. 22 (London: James Duncan, 1830), 417–418 quoted in Stephen Holmes, *God of Grace and God of Glory: An Account of the Theology of Jonathan Edwards* (Grand Rapids: William B. Eerdmans Publishing Company, 2001), 205.

184. John Wesley, *Wesley's Notes on the Bible*, 422.

185. Alexander Campbell, *Popular Lectures and Addresses*, 449.

186. Alexander Campbell, *Popular Lectures and Addresses*, 421.

187. Richard Baxter, *Works* vol. 22 (London: James Duncan, 1830), 419 quoted in Stephen Holmes, *God of Grace and God of Glory: An Account of the Theology of Jonathan Edwards*, 205.

188. Brigham Young in *Journal of Discourses*, 16:42.

189. Joseph Smith, *The Words of Joseph Smith*, 14.

190. Joseph Smith, *HC*, 3:389–390.

191. Joseph Smith, *The Words of Joseph Smith*, 113.

192. There are many places in scripture where the Lord refers to this truth conceptually. He does so when he describes Himself as Alpha and Omega (Revelation 1:11; 22:13; 3 Nephi 9:18; D&C 38:1; 107:19) or the first and the last (Isaiah 41:4; see also Revelation 3:14; D&C 110:4).

193. Smith, *History of the Church*, 2:52.

194. Ibid., 3:30.

195. Ibid., 1:98.

196. Dallin H. Oaks "Powerful Ideas" *Ensign*, November 1995, 26.

197. Ibid.

About the Author

Chad Morris is a seminary teacher and EFY speaker. He received a Master's Degree in Religious Education from Brigham Young University, writing his thesis on the subject of this book. Chad currently resides in Kaysville, Utah, with his wife, Shelly. They have four young children, including one-year-old identical twin boys.